# GLIMPSES OF THE ETERNAL

## THE INNER LAW

ACHARYA SITARAMA BRAHMAM P



BlueRose ONE.com
Stories Matter
NewDelhi • London

**BLUEROSE PUBLISHERS**
India | U.K.



For permissions requests or inquiries regarding this publication, please contact:

BLUEROSE PUBLISHERS
www.BlueRoseONE.com
info@bluerosepublishers.com
+91 8882 898 898
+4407342408967

ISBN: 978-93-7139-239-6

Cover design: Yash Singhal
Typesetting: Namrata Saini

First Edition: October 2025

# Dedication

*To the wayfarers who tread the luminous path of Truth*
*To the restless minds seeking wisdom beyond the seen*
*To the hearts that resonate with the*
*Silent whispers of the Infinite*
*And to the Souls yearning to dissolve*
*Into the embrace of the Eternal*

# Acknowledgements

This book is the fruit of a profound Spiritual Legacy, entrusted to us for preservation and dissemination. We, the editors, express our deepest reverence to Acharya P. Sitaramabrahmam, whose wisdom continues to illuminate seekers across generations.

We are immensely grateful to Prof. Amina Kishore for her unwavering support, insightful suggestions, and invaluable contributions in bringing this edition to life. Her encouragement and thoughtful inputs have enriched the essence of this work.

May this effort serve its purpose in guiding those who seek the Eternal truth.

*Ilyas Ahmed*

*Dr Jyothsna Ilyas*

*Dr Asma Ahmed*

Editors

2025

# Contents

# Foreword

To encounter a teacher who not only imparts wisdom but also awakens the depths of one's Soul is a rare blessing. Acharya P. Sitarama Brahmam was such a guide in my life—a mentor whose profound insights and Faith illuminated my own path toward ministry and a deeper engagement with the Brahmo Faith. His teachings did not merely instruct; they kindled a fire of inquiry, urging one to seek beyond the transient and glimpse the Eternal.

Glimpses of the Eternal is not a book in the conventional sense. It is a call to reflection, a mirror held up to the Soul. In its pages, Acharya Sitarama Brahmam does not offer dogma, nor does he demand blind adherence to it. Instead, he invites us to wrestle with the fundamental questions of existence—questions that have perplexed seekers across ages yet remain as urgent today as ever. In an era where the sacred is often drowned out by the clamour of material pursuits, where virtue is dismissed as archaic, and where Faith itself is challenged at every turn, these writings offer not just solace but direction. They remind us that the Divine is not a distant ideal but a living Presence within us, waiting to be awakened. Acharya Sitarama Brahmam understood that Faith is not about retreating from the world but about transforming it by infusing our daily lives with a higher purpose and by bridging the chasm between the ideal and the real.

The themes explored in this book—the need for the Divine, the role of Faith, and the power of Spiritual Inspiration—are not abstract musings. They are deeply practical, for they speak to the human condition, our struggles, and our yearnings. This work is a reminder that righteousness is not sustained by mere laws or social conventions but by an inner awakening, an alignment with the sacred order that permeates existence. Faith, however, is not a passive state of belief; it is an active, living force. As Acharya Sitarama Brahmam profoundly states, Faith in the Divine is not the same as Faith in the mere idea of the Divine. The former is a living confidence in an Ever-Present, guiding force; the latter is an intellectual convenience, an abstract affirmation of something greater without a transformative relationship.

True Faith is a deep trust in the unfolding path, a commitment to living in harmony with it, and an unshakable certainty that the Universe moves with purpose and meaning. Such Faith is cultivated, not inherited. It is nourished through experience, deepened through prayer, and strengthened by surrender to the greater Will. Yet, remaining steadfast in Faith requires strength of character. The path to true Faith is obstructed by attachment to transient values, by distractions, and by the ever-present lure of the ego. To persevere, one must remind oneself: "*The Sacred Presence is my refuge and companion, my unseen support through all difficulties.*"

For the seeker who yearns for a world where the Spiritual and the temporal are not in conflict but in harmony, Glimpses of the Eternal is both an invitation and a challenge. It is both an invitation to discover the infinite potential within and a challenge to rise above the transient, embracing the Eternal. It is a call to Faith, not merely in an abstract Divine Presence, but in the ever-guiding force of the Sacred. It is a call to awaken, to illuminate the world with the Light of Truth, and to journey the path of righteousness with courage, wisdom, and an unshakable trust in the unfolding Sacred Design. May these pages inspire all who turn them to walk the path of Truth with conviction and Faith, for in doing so, we glimpse the Eternal.

With deep reverence and gratitude,

**Rev. Abhi Janamanchi**

**Senior Minister, Cedar Lane Unitarian Universalist Congregation, Bethesda, Maryland, USA**

# Preface

A disquietude hangs heavy in the air of our modern age. The sanctity of human life seems to be eroding, its value diminishing with each passing day. Culture, once a beacon of light, now flickers uncertainly, sometimes obscuring rather than illuminating the path ahead. Morality, a cherished melody of the past, is met with derision. Virtue offers little solace to the weary Soul. In the frenzied clamour of progress, we seem to have forgotten the sacred rhythm that once harmonised our existence with the Eternal.

Yet, amidst this prevailing darkness, a flicker of hope persists. It speaks of a more Profound Truth waiting to be discovered, one that promises a Life brimming with immense potential. Our true dignity lies not in emulating the baser instincts of the animal kingdom but in awakening the Divine Essence that exists within each of us. Once awakened, this Essence must become the driving force of our lives, a luminous thread guiding us through the maze of existence. The Ideal must elevate the ordinary, and the ordinary, in turn, must strive to embody the Ideal. An Ideal that dwells solely in the realm of dreams offers fleeting solace. In contrast, a reality devoid of Ideal descends into barbarity—a state we tragically see spreading across the globe, eroding the very foundations of our shared Humanity.

The ideas within this book are not mere pronouncements but the culmination of a lifelong quest for a world infused with a sense of the Divine, a 'Heavenly Earth'. These thoughts, born of personal reflection and the struggles of the human spirit, are offered as companions to fellow seekers navigating the thorny path of life. The journey may be fraught with challenges, but it is illuminated by the promise of a brighter tomorrow. In this world, the spark of Divinity transforms despair into hope and chaos into harmony.

This book does not propose a utopia detached from reality, nor does it seek to dismiss the struggles of the present. Instead, it offers a way to reconcile the Ideal with the practical, urging us to weave the threads of aspiration into the fabric of our everyday lives. To transform our existence is not a task for the faint-hearted; it demands courage, Faith, and an unwavering commitment to rise above the transient and embrace the Eternal.

If these pages speak to you, let them be a companion on your own quiet quest for meaning. They are offered not as answers but as sparks—glimpses that may kindle your own insight and deepen your sense of life's wonder. May they remind you that within the ordinary moments of living lie hidden treasures, waiting for the one who pauses long enough to see. May they, as gentle messengers, whisper that even in the plainest hour, the Infinite leans close, awaiting our recognition.

**- Acharya Sitaramabrahmam P**

# CHAPTER 1

# The Need for God and The God We Need

In human existence, there is a dramatic interplay among three powerful forces: the State, Society, and the Concept of God. Each of these forces shapes the moral evolution of individuals and communities, depending on how it functions and the degree to which people respond to its influence.

The role of the Government is to monitor and regulate human behaviour through correction, warning, and punishment, utilising its tools, which include laws, courts, prisons, police, and military. It issues a series of commands, such as *Dos* and *Don'ts.* While it recognises and rewards select individuals, such gestures are symbolic and secondary to its primary focus: maintenance of order. Yet governance often mirrors the shortcomings of Society—ignorance, fear, and selfishness—rendering it a flawed and insensitive instrument.

Philosophers and visionaries, from Karl Marx to Sri Aurobindo, have envisioned futures without Government or with evolved forms of human Society. Sri Aurobindo even visualised the emergence of a superior human race through the arrival of a higher Consciousness on Earth. Yet from a practical standpoint, such ideals may often appear utopian. It remains evident that humanity requires some form of governance—an external structure of control and discipline—to live righteously. One can easily picture the chaos and anarchy that would prevail without it.

The Government, though indispensable, remains limited in its usefulness. It prioritises order over transformation, appearance over Truth, and cannot awaken the moral core of man. Its punitive methods are not foolproof, as evidence can be manipulated, and justice often eludes the innocent. In short, it is a mechanical structure devoid of moral impulse, emphasising the letter of the Law while ignoring its spirit. The Law of the land may restrain the hand, but it cannot restrain the heart. True righteousness does not arise from fear of punishment or desire for reward, but from the innate desire in humans to be considered just, good, and noble in the eyes of others. Is there a greater reward than seeing respect for us in the eyes of others or being honoured by Society? And is there a greater pain than being disowned by friends—or worse, dismissed as an errant or misfit by the very community in which one lives?

The inherent desire for validation or praise from one's own community is more liberating than any decree, and a looming fear of disapproval is more binding than any statute. This subtle pressure, rooted not in enforcement but in belonging, awakens an Inner Law—one that governs from within. Once awakened, it becomes an existential reality: a force that shapes man's values, fuels his conscience, and aligns him with the greater good.

## The Influence of Society

So, the second force shaping man's moral growth is Society. Its influence is more far-reaching than that of Government, for it extends beyond outward actions to the very fabric of thought and feeling. Humans are inherently social and cannot live in isolation; their social environment shapes their thoughts, feelings, habits, sentiments, and ideals.

Unlike the Government, which punishes misdeeds with a prison sentence, Society judges individuals on a deeper level, guided not by statutes but by morality, traditions, and conventions, imposing a far harsher penalty. The fear of tarnished reputation and social persecution imposes a powerful moral pressure—one that reaches beyond the individual to their family and descendants. No decree of law compares to the sting of ridicule or the yearning for communal respect. This subtle but persistent societal influence is a powerful force that shapes our moral compass more profoundly than punishment ever could.

The customs and conventions of social life—absent in the acts of Government—shape behaviour profoundly. Prestige, respectability, and the need for harmonious relations foster a moral sense in man. From this perspective, Society's standards of good and evil, right and wrong, and its strictures surpass those of the Government.

Yet Society, though a cohesive force, has its own limitations. Public opinion and social relations are often shaped by inconsistent or questionable tenets that are uncritically inherited from tradition or folklore. As a result, Society tends to resist what lies beyond its established norms, failing to grasp values or ideas that challenge its comfort zone or exceed its past experience. History bears witness through the lives of Prophets and Reformers who were often met with suspicion or outright hostility. Even among the intellectual elite, few dare to confront convention or defy collective opinion, despite recognising its superficiality. Such reluctance to question inherited norms underscores the need for individual moral growth, one that transcends the artificial constructs of societal approval.

Society's moral fabric is mostly uniform, often reflecting the same collective confusions—fear, superstition, and resistance to the new. Therefore, prevailing public opinion lacks the depth and discernment necessary to exert a meaningful moral influence. Clouded by misconceptions and unfounded fears, the collective conscience cannot serve as a guiding force for higher ethical standards, rendering Society an inadequate measure of true moral progress. Social recognition is not proof of inner nobility; one may feign upright conduct while harbouring contrary thoughts or leading a secret, unprincipled life. Even the most distinguished Society may fail to lead men to ethical perfection.

Society, though evolved, remains bound by the memory of its own past. Its codes, customs, and reputations are mirrors—sometimes clear, sometimes warped—of collective experience, not individual conscience. While it can discipline behaviour through fear or approval, it cannot compel transformation. No applause can awaken virtue; no censure alone can elevate the Soul. The need for a deeper awakening arises when social expectations cease to hold meaning for the inwardly seeking individual.

Yet beyond the reach of judgment and public consequence, a quiet force calls us inward—the voice of Truth untouched by societal measure. It is here, in the stillness of the Soul, that morality ceases to be imposed and begins to be revealed. A whisper not of what is expected, but of what is Eternally right.

## Power of Divine Inspiration

Our actions are not always driven by material gain or coercion. Often, we are inspired to do things close to our hearts for the sheer delight of self-expression. This inner necessity produces pioneering and valuable work. This inspiration manifests in patriotism, humanitarianism, philanthropy, poetry, scientific discoveries, and fine arts. Prophets, scientists, creative artists, and poets are neither produced by the State nor trained by Society. A person afire with such inspiration is selfless and fearless, defying societal norms and Government laws that hinder human progress. He endeavours to usher in higher values. Divine inspiration, arising from higher planes of Consciousness, reveals the secrets of Nature and the mysteries of the Universe. Such an individual transcends the need for external laws. He aligns with the deeper *Laws of Being* that surpass external codes. This discovery is possible through attunement to a Truth above the mind, which we call God.

God, or Universal Energy, is an inexhaustible reservoir of all that is worthy and precious, which guides individuals and nations to higher stages of evolution—materially, intellectually, morally, and spiritually. This Universal Energy may manifest directly or mystically. A conscious effort and integration of one's inner personality are essential to tap into it. God is the All-Pervading, Eternal, and Perfect Ideal that encompasses and transcends all other ideals. His Energy urges us to live wisely and boldly, maintaining peace amidst fluctuating fortunes, and provides solace during agonising times. It leads us to understand the Truth and the Nature of Truth. It also lets us realise that every immediate Truth is linked to the Ultimate Truth. The sense of separation, selfishness, death, fear, and sorrow can be overcome by realising our Eternal Unity with all. This realisation that we are undying Spiritual Realities, in harmony with all, is part of God-Realisation. Only through alignment with God's Energy does our destiny mature along twin dimensions: an ascent toward the Divine and an extension into the world.

## Deception in the name of God

But even this sacred current, when filtered through human desire and fear, risks distortion, its clarity clouded, its purity redirected. The idea of God, like all potent forces, has not escaped this fate. Across centuries, man has wrapped Divinity in the robes of ambition, cast Him in the contours of prejudice, and summoned His Name to serve private ends.

The sacred has been institutionalised, commercialised, even bartered—as though God were a negotiable asset. This distortion has sanctioned cruelty and cloaked injustice in righteousness; pages of religious history run crimson with the consequences.

A radical shift in mindset could perhaps change this situation. Yet a mere horizontal conversion cannot bring renewal, for it means nothing more than shifting allegiance from one creed, sect, or label to another—a sideways motion without growth, like circling endlessly over the same rugged ground. Vertical conversion, by contrast, is ascent: the deepening of conscience, the inward turning that transcends labels and rituals, and the rising toward genuine *Spiritual Awakening*.

A man is not defined by the religious denomination he inherits, but by his inner battle with darkness—his triumph over the beast and the devil within. A true conception of God must stir the heart toward kinship with all beings and reverence for Truth. If it fails to do so—if it cannot awaken the Divine spark or safeguard what is noble—it stands not as a beacon, but as a danger.

Yet even amid confusion, the Soul remains restless for what is Real. Beneath the layers of falsehood, there stirs a yearning that neither the State nor Society can satisfy—a longing for the Sacred that cannot be politicised, or made to serve ambition. When all else fails to inspire transformation, the Soul turns inward, seeking a Faith that is not borrowed but born from within—a living flame of Realisation that guides the Soul beyond all external doctrines.

# CHAPTER 2

# Why Faith?

We live in times fraught with paradox. The old is discarded, age-old certainties dismantled, and cherished values interrogated with relentless scepticism. As desires multiply, the intricacies of life's problems escalate, weaving a denser web of complications. Frustrations mount, mental illnesses rise, and breakdowns are increasingly commonplace. The insatiable demand for sedatives, alcohol, and narcotics feeds this chaos, while suicides, once rare, are now tragically prevalent.

Science and technology, heralded as the pinnacles of human achievement, have bestowed unprecedented power on man. Yet, this untamed power, much like Frankenstein's monster—conceived with brilliance, yet unleashed without wisdom—is now turning against its maker. An unbalanced mind might use such power as a perilous weapon, and if this trend persists unchecked, anarchy and chaos will inevitably ensue. It is crucial to promptly discern the root causes of these afflictions and address them with clarity and purpose to prevent such a fate.

## Faith: The Hidden Axis of Life

*What underlies our daily actions?* Rarely do we pause to pose this question. We remain oblivious to its profundity, preoccupied with peripheral matters while neglecting the intimate core of our existence. Just as the eye observes all but itself and the mind recalls thoughts without questioning their origin, so too do we overlook the silent axis that guides our lives.

How do we make our day-to-day choices and act upon them? Do we meticulously analyse, calculate, and deliberate before every decision? Certainly not. Life's rhythm flows without constant scrutiny. We reason only when disruptions demand it; otherwise, we move spontaneously. What does this reveal?

This spontaneity rests on an implicit trust in life's continuity—an integral trust that often goes unnoticed. This silent force is Faith. It is not deliberate but instinctive, deeply embedded in the fabric of our being. When we go to bed, we have no doubts about whether we will wake up the next day. The occasional news that we hear of death in sleep does not disturb our trust; we consider them as exceptions to the general rule. This Faith sustains our confidence in the rhythm of life and the reliability of natural laws.

We trust the sunrise each morning and the sunset in the evening, and we also trust that the seasons change precisely from one to the other. At a general level, we place our health in the hands of doctors, our disputes before judges, and our children under the care of teachers, even though we know that doctors, judges, or teachers are not infallible. Faith is the unseen bond connecting us to Life's flow, an unshakable assurance in the continuity of 'order'.

Faith rests upon our inherent awareness of an unyielding Law that governs the universe. There is an unerring rhythm in the past, present, and future. In the sequence of bud, blossom, and fruit, the progression is infallible—no flower regresses to a bud, and no fruit transforms back into a flower. The immutable order unfolds potential into reality.

An expectant mother preparing a cradle for her unborn child, the farmer sowing seeds, the teacher enlightening the pupil, the reformer enduring persecution, and an idealist dedicating his life to his ideals—all draw strength from their Faith in this Law. Without it, science would have no foundation for discovery, and life would become chaotic. This Law, inseparable from its Giver, affirms the Divine Harmony underlying existence.

## The Cornerstone of Righteousness

True religion transforms instinctive Faith into conscious, purposeful belief, awakening its latent power to shape destiny. As the Sanskrit adage declares, *'Vishwaaso Dharma Moolam'*—Faith is the root of righteousness. It is the starting point, the root of Spiritual life.

Like the grammar of language, the foundation of a building, or the root of a tree, Faith is indispensable for religion.

*"Let none proclaim Faith who has not lit its flame within; for when the hour of darkness falls, only the inwardly kindled shall walk unshaken."* — *Inspired by the Upanishadic spirit.*

Temptations abound in the path of life, and storms are many. Those who encounter them without Faith shall surely fall. No matter how much one may pride oneself on wisdom, virtue, or piety, these alone are insufficient against the tempests of existence. For it is Faith that serves as the unshakable foundation upon which true strength and resilience must be built. Without this firm ground to uphold them, even the loftiest ideals crumble, and the house of life, deprived of its sustaining pillar, is destined to collapse into ruin. A life built on the rock of True Faith shall not give way even if roaring surges beat against it.

## The Nature of True Faith

What is Faith? It is not an opinion, intellectual belief, or agreement based on an age-old tradition, nor is it acceptance due to the majority behind it. Nor is it based on respect because great men sanctioned it, honouring out of fear, or following because of some advantage. It is not a lack of belief in anybody or anything. Faith is not fatalism or superstition. Faith is not passive.

Faith is a faculty and power of the Soul. It has foresight and insight. It sees beyond the present and beneath the surface. As conscience is the ear of the Soul, Faith is the eye of the Soul. Faith is the sixth sense; it is the evidence of things unseen. We walk by Faith, not sight, for Faith sees farther than sight.

The effects of Prayer are more psychological than physical, and without Faith, Prayer is a hollow gesture, stagnating Spiritual growth. Thomas Watson, a 17th-century English Puritan preacher, said, *"Without Faith, it is speaking, not praying. Faith is the breath of Prayer; Prayer is dead unless Faith breathes in it."*

In Faith, there is no place for words like '*may,*' '*perhaps,*' '*probably,*' '*if,*' or '*but.*'

*"O God, if you really exist, if I have a Soul, if you can help it, please help me out of my difficulties."* Since such Prayers reflect a total lack of Faith in the existence and power of the All-Pervading God and the Soul, they can never be fulfilled.

What instinct is to the birds and beasts, and logic to the intellect, Faith is to the Soul. It is a force that can transform the impossible into the attainable, achieving the miraculous. The lives of the great and wise stand as eloquent testaments to this Truth. When circumstances disappoint, wealth, power, and worldly pomp fail, and darkness and despair encircle the spirit, Faith alone sustains—an indomitable strength within the heart and a radiant light upon the path.

Faith is a quiet force that engenders detachment and independence and is a harbinger of optimism. While reason appeals to a fragment of man, Faith addresses the totality of his being. Reason, though indispensable, lacks the alchemy to transform human nature unless it works in harmony with a disciplined and consenting Soul. All philosophical arguments, the cosmological, the ontological, the teleological, and the moral, may seek to affirm the existence of God—yet, restless and sceptical, the inquirer's mind persists in its query: *Is God real?*

Reason is vital for dispelling superstition, interpreting experience, and codifying truths. Yet, intelligence, aspiration, and learning must rest upon the bedrock of Faith. The absence of Faith reveals a mind that is rigid, crude, and insensitive, incapable of perceiving the finer whispers of Truth. Faith is not opposed to reason; it transcends it. Faith is the rudder of life, essential for both righteous living and Spiritual ascent.

The Spiritual Journey is fraught with doubts, difficulties, and discouragements, far greater than those encountered in worldly pursuits. These obstacles are often internal, arising from the depths of one's being.

## Faith in God

One cannot speak of Faith in God casually, for it is not merely Faith in the idea of God, but in God Himself. The distinction is profound. Faith in the idea of God is an intellectual convenience, a preference for the notion of God's existence over doubt or denial. It is a belief in a higher power, a force that guides and shapes the universe. Faith in God, however, is a living confidence in His direct relationship, His methods, and His providence. It is a personal, experiential relationship with the Divine, a trust in His wisdom and love.

While Faith in the idea of God may suffice for propagating doctrines and building institutions, True Faith is not just a belief in the existence of a higher power, but a deep trust in the Divine Plan and a commitment to living in harmony with it. It embraces confidence in oneself, one's latent Divinity, and the evolutionary march of life. It is a resolute assertion of man's sovereignty over his desires and the objects of desire.

Faith is a quiet yet unyielding certainty, even amidst daunting adversities—a steadfast assurance of an approaching dawn despite the enveloping night. Where there is True Faith, there is no room for hesitation or compromise.

Faith, like all faculties, must be cultivated through practice and experience. It is not a passive belief but an active force that nourishes and grows. Prayer and meditation nourish Faith, infusing vitality into our Spiritual Journey. The pursuit of Spiritual Ideals provides the fertile ground for Faith's growth. Yet, Faith must harmonise with surrender to the Divine Will; insistence upon one's desires and egoistic demands contradicts the essence of Faith. It is a commitment, a journey, and a way of life.

However, while cultivating Faith requires clarity and discipline, remaining in Faith requires strength of character and conviction.

The primary causes of falling out of Faith are attachments to transient values, allegiance to false deities, and the dominance of bodily instincts and egoistic impulses. To grow in Faith, one must cultivate humility, surrender to the Divine, and have an expansive vision that embraces unity with all. Amidst trials, the aspirant must remind himself: *I am an Eternal spark of the Divine. God is my refuge and companion, my unseen support through all difficulties. In His wisdom, He shares my burdens and leads me through life's ordeals. I am in His company.*

One readily trusts planetary influences, palmistry, or self-styled godmen, who are often rife with ignorance and frailty. Yet, one finds it arduous to trust the one true God, who is closer than his breath and remains an unfailing guide, Eternal companion, and Omniscient friend.

In a world chasing fleeting truths, it is Faith in the Eternal that anchors man—and beckons him home. Without Faith in the true God, man becomes a wanderer in the labyrinth of life, rushing from one false refuge to another, only to find himself ensnared in his illusions.

# CHAPTER 3

# The Goal and the Direction

Today, humanity finds itself in the midst of tumultuous upheavals, where the sanctity of Life is disregarded and human values desecrated. Though we bask in the triumphs of science and the splendours of technology, peace eludes us still. Our achievements echo hollowly, for the spirit of fraternity is all but forgotten.

The ideal of harmonious coexistence—*"live and let live"*—has become a mere cliché, honoured more in breach than in practice. The march of progress appears to lead not to Enlightenment but towards the precipice of peril, as the tools of destruction grow ever more refined, threatening the very safety and sanctity of ordinary existence.

From where does this malady spring? Why does this dark shadow linger over the march of civilisation? To discern the origin of this malevolent shadow is to undertake a journey towards clarity, for no darkness can be dispelled without first unravelling the confusion of thought. We must pierce through the veils of appearance to the Truth of things, linking the proximate to the Ultimate, the fleeting to the Eternal.

Only by moving from the known to the unknown may we find the compass that points to humanity's liberation.

Man, a social being, is bound to the Society that nurtures him. Society is not merely a collection of individuals but a complex web of relationships and their influence. Every influence a man receives—direct or subtle—has its roots in this collective.

However, from a Spiritual perspective, the body is woven from Universal matter; the breath is a ripple in the vast ocean of life; the Mind is a fragment of Cosmic Intelligence. Thus, man does not stand apart but participates in the *Grand Symphony of Existence.* In its infinite vastness, the Universe is his actual Society, and Nature, in all her abundance, is his Eternal Ally.

## One, the Origin of All

Whether matter or spirit, all that is, originates in the One. From this One, all beings emerge; in it, they are sustained, and to it, they ultimately return. The brotherhood of man is not a fanciful invention of idealists, nor an empty slogan—but an Eternal Truth rooted in the indivisible Unity of Existence.

Just as the pain of an injured limb reverberates through the entire body, so does the suffering or upliftment of one individual echo across the collective. Man's thoughts, words, or actions send ripples across this interconnected web of life. A mystic kinship exists between the stars that gleam in the heavens and the flowers that bloom on Earth, for all are bound by the same Law of Unity.

The ideas of the Great Ones continue to influence humanity with unmitigated vigour and vitality, echoing across centuries. An event in one corner of the Universe has chain reactions throughout.

The Bhagavad Gita reminds us of this Truth: "*His hands and feet are everywhere; His eyes, ears, and faces pervade the Cosmos. This Eternal One—the Source and Substance of all things—abides in every form and formlessness, manifesting as the manifold, and as the many within the One.*"

## Unity and Harmony

For Religion to serve as a corrective and purifying force in public life, its social dimension must be emphasised. For too long, humanity has partitioned existence into the Spiritual (*paaramarthika*) and the mundane (*vyaavahaarika*), as though sundering the head from the body.

This dichotomy has bred hypocrisy, reducing spirituality to ritual and secular life to moral chaos.

Such a separation injures the Truth, which encompasses both the Spiritual and the Material as inner and outer aspects. Most of our lives are spent in worldly activities and interactions with others. Without a guiding force, these aspects of life are vulnerable to satanic influences. Humanism, devoid of a Spiritual foundation, is but a fragile edifice. Living in harmony with these ideals transforms the mundane into the Sublime and guides humanity towards the flowering of its Divine Potential.

The most profound Truth lies in the Unity of Existence and the harmony of relationships. Life's purpose is not fulfilled in isolation nor conflict but in the interplay of the one and the many, each enriching the other. The Cosmic Cycles unfold the many from the One and return the many to their origin in an Eternal dance of Unity. *"Each for all, and all for each"*, is the guiding principle of this Universal Harmony. To deviate from this Law is to court chaos; to align with it is to move toward perfection.

Man is deeply indebted to Nature and Society for all he receives—the air he breathes, the sustenance he enjoys, and the knowledge he inherits. He must live in a way that honours this debt, maintaining the harmony of the larger whole. Any exploitation beyond legitimate needs invites inevitable retribution. Trees may silently endure the axe, but a world denuded of forests would spell doom for humanity. This Law extends to all forms of exploitation; for Nature's patience, though vast, is not without limit.

The exploitation of the weak and innocent cannot go unpunished either. Evil carries within it the seed of its own destruction. Cruelty and selfishness reverberate through life, returning to their source with multiplied force.

God cannot be reached by hating fellow beings, nor is Heaven attained by creating a hell on Earth.

*"He who sees himself in others and others in himself is liberated"*, say the *Upanishads*—for such vision dissolves the walls of separation.

## True Essence of Religion

Popular beliefs and practices in all religions often contradict the spirit of their founders' fundamental teachings. The mission to realign Religion with its original purity and Universal Essence requires the instrument of Spiritual discernment and Religious rationalism, accepting the basic concepts of Religion as axioms and also rediscovering their Eternal Beauty.

Religion in its essence is one, Universal and Indivisible. While the practices and symbols may vary, the spirit behind them is the same. A unified Faith, embracing the One, is a source of Eternal Beauty and Joy.

Sectarianism, by contrast, breeds bigotry and strife. It fragments the Truth, reducing the infinite to the narrow confines of exclusivity. The *Upanishads* urge us to transcend this limitation and see all as One and One as all.

There are three standpoints to Truth: *"This is true"*; *"This alone is true"*; and *"This alone is not true"*. The viewpoint *that this alone is not true* leads to a Universal outlook and synthesis, whereas the view that *"this alone is true"* generates ill feelings and contempt.

This leads us to the diverse religions in our world—and the need for understanding the essence of true Religion.

True Faith is not inherited but realised. It cannot be passed down as a mere tradition but must be lived and experienced. However, in the curious world of religious inheritance, many people identify with a particular religion simply because they were born into it. A child of a Christian is called a Christian, even if they have questions about the Divinity of Christ. A child of a Muslim is considered a Muslim, even if he has not fully embraced all the tenets of Islam. A child of a Hindu proudly identifies as a Hindu, even if unfamiliar with the intricacies of Hinduism, yet enjoys its festivals and traditions.

True Faith requires understanding the principles, wholeheartedly accepting them for personal fulfilment, and living by them. Being born into a religion is the starting point, not the entirety of the journey. The journey of Faith begins with understanding, matures in acceptance, and culminates in *Self-Transcendence.*

*Is our Faith within us or outside us?* If it is within us, is it assimilated or unassimilated? If unassimilated, it may help give discourses and sermons to others. If assimilated as a part of our Nature, it becomes a Strength and a Light on our path.

The concept of God and the way of Worship should transcend creeds, dogmas, traditions, and denominations. God is not confined to institutions, rituals, or doctrines. He dwells in the silent depths of the Soul, guiding everyone toward the realisation of their Divine Possibilities.

Let us seek Him not in the shadows of division but in the Radiance of Unity, aspiring for a life that reflects the infinite beauty of His Truth.

## Beyond Institutions

An institution is not God, nor can loyalty to an institution replace devotion to Him. While institutions are valuable and necessary, they have limitations. One must understand their value and limitations, eventually outgrow them, and embrace true Faith.

True Faith is an attitude and a way of life. The core of this Faith lies in using Prayer to address personal problems, fulfil inner needs, derive strength and comfort, cultivate broader sympathies, and grow in the Image of the Divine. An adherent should exemplify integrity, develop a strong inner personality, help others, and contribute to the greater good.

# CHAPTER 4

# Religion

Since the primordial dawn of human awakening, man's heart has been illuminated by an inextinguishable flame—a sacred instinct for the Infinite, a silent yet imperious call to Transcendence. Assailed by storms of ignorance and shadows of doubt, this Divine hunger endures—unyielding and Eternal. Beneath the fevered surface of life's ceaseless striving lies a profound homesickness: a haunting awareness that we are not mere momentary figures etched upon the sands of time, but wanderers destined for an abiding Truth, in search of Greater Light.

This whisper of the Infinite—subtle as a breath, yet potent as a clarion—summons the Soul to ascend beyond the limits of mortal being and rediscover its luminous origins. Yet man, fumbling and unenlightened, weaves around this sacred aspiration a web of half-truths and transient certainties. These fragile constructs—like fleeting mirages in a desert—promise solace, but fail to satiate the thirst they pretend to quench. And the unrelieved Soul continues its silent yearning, untouched by the satisfactions of outer life.

From this deep yearning, coupled with the mind's inherent inability to grasp the ineffable, arises a kaleidoscope of paradigms—dogmas, superstitions, and boundless flights of imagination. Each presents itself as the ultimate path to fulfil the Soul's Eternal longing, yet most serve only to divide and fragment the Spirit of humanity. Religions have emerged in countless forms, fashioning heavens and hells of infinite variety—each shaped by the vision, or the limitations, of those who conceived them. While these Faiths offer profound promises and forge communities bound by devotion, they also reinforce divisions.

The dogmas that ignite fervour in one group breed suspicion or hostility in another. Even the ideal of tolerance—*"live and let live"*—is practised not from understanding but as an uneasy compromise, a truce rather than a Truth.

Coexistence becomes a mechanism of necessity, while deeper disunity festers in the human psyche—a subtle but insidious veil that obstructs the realisation of Oneness.

Thus, humanity, bound by the compulsions of practicality, collaborates outwardly but remains inwardly fragmented, caught in the ceaseless rhythm of division and striving.

Though the call to Transcendence is clear and persistent, it is muffled in the cacophony of separative thought. Yet the Soul's cry remains Eternal and unquenchable, awaiting man's awakening to a higher Unity—a Luminous Truth beyond creed and construct, beyond shadow and flame.

## The True Soul of Religion

The learned in every tradition often interpret popular beliefs, lending them dignity and intellectual weight. Yet rarely do they pause to question the inconsistencies they uphold. Instead of introspection, there is rationalisation; instead of reform, reinforcement. Pride in tradition is elevated above the pursuit of Truth, and their endorsement gives these ideas stature and status, fostering self-importance in their adherents.

Propaganda and canvassing are carried out with holy zeal to demonstrate the superiority of one's beliefs over others. Ill feelings and jealousy fuel this missionary zeal. Conversions are pursued with competitive fervour.

The frenzy does not end there. Over time, people belonging to the same Faith splinter into sects. Not only is Religion, in a broader sense, codified and systematised, but even these sects become rigid and airtight to insulate themselves from external influences.

Enlightened individuals—revered as Avatars, Prophets, or Messengers of the Divine—have appeared throughout history to guide humanity, illuminating the deeper significance of inner restlessness and the pursuit of higher aspirations.

However, people entrenched in fantastical beliefs and traditions are often unmoved by mere philosophy and reasoning, even when it appeals to the intellect. Rational explanations alone rarely leave a lasting impact. Instead, it is those who demonstrate extraordinary powers or miracles that inspire devotion and command true influence over their followers.

The Law of Evolution suggests that Perfection is its ultimate goal. Humanity's hopes and anxious efforts are struggles in ignorance towards Perfection. This Perfection already resides within, like a mighty tree slumbering in a seed. Drawn upward by an invisible pull, it compels us toward our highest possibility. In this inner propulsion lies the Soul of Religion and the secret meaning of Life. This longing for Perfection is inherent to human nature and shared by all humankind. Even after understanding this, the entrenched associations of beliefs, practices, and creeds unique to each group persist with stubborn tenacity.

At its core, Religion is both Universal and singular. Many people confuse it with its outward forms and superficial aspects. Few seek the true substance, and even fewer strive for the true Soul of Religion. At the heart of Religion lies man's movement towards Perfection and the idea of God reaching out to man. It calls for man's complete, active, and integrated cooperation, which is crucial for fulfilling God's plan.

## An Ideal Prayer

Out of the persistent movement toward Perfection arises a deep and wordless longing, often welling up in the human heart—a yearning not for possession but for release from bondage, from fragmentation, from the weight of the ego. This yearning finds its most natural expression in Prayer—not a conventional petition for worldly favours, but a Soul's quiet invocation for liberation, transformation, and union. In this quiet imploring lies one of the most direct and sacred paths to the Divine.

The devotee's Prayer should not be a clamour for ephemeral gains but a Soul's earnest cry for liberation:

*'Lift me out of these limitations; free me from this bondage; break these fetters that confine me to boundaries.'*

What are these fetters? They are the heavy chains of *Tamas*, the inertia of the body, the fiery bonds of *Rajas*, the restlessness of desire, envy, and domination, and the persistent grip of mental egoism. The genuine aspiration is to transcend these lower tendencies and rise into the realm of Divine Light, Peace, and Dynamic Harmony. Liberation is found in transcending the egoic sense of separation and merging into the Oneness of all Existence.

The transformation of the *Gunas—Sattva*, *Rajas*, and *Tamas*—into their Divine counterparts is perhaps the very essence of Spiritual Evolution.

Prayer, if it is to bear fruit, must be rooted in the soil of Faith, watered by sincerity, and illumined by earnestness. Faith is the Soul's assurance of its Divine destiny; Prayer without Faith is an empty shell. Sincerity, free from divided loyalties, aligns the heart with the Spirit's single aim. Earnestness lends movement to sincerity, and intensity propels the aspirant to heights beyond the ordinary reach. To pray effectively, one integrates thought, speech, and action into a harmonious rhythm that resonates with the Divine ideal.

## Prayer and Grace

Prayer is the vital force that bridges the finite and the Infinite, the mortal and the Immortal, transmuting the Soul through the subtle alchemy of Divine Grace. Prayer rises as a cry from the depths of man's being, a call from below; Grace is its Celestial answer, descending from above as a shower of Light and Benediction. In this sacred interplay lies the axis of Spiritual Existence. It is an indescribable dialogue yet profound: man reaches out in supplication, and God listens; God whispers, and man hearkens. Through steadfast, fervent, and unwavering engagement, Prayer evolves into Communion—culminating in silent absorption. At this pinnacle, the human Soul, once fettered by its limitations, soars into the vastness of the Divine, losing itself only to find its most authentic self.

## The Journey to Perfection

The Universal Quest for perfection testifies to humanity's being in a continual state of *becoming*, a work in progress, ever striving toward its destined realisation. Perfection is not an external achievement, but an internal liberation—a realisation of the Divinity that lies dormant within each of us.

As Swami Vivekananda eloquently puts it, *"Each Soul is potentially Divine. The goal is to manifest this Divine within by controlling nature—external and internal."*

The paths to Spiritual Awakening are diverse and manifold—work, Worship, psychological discipline, and knowledge—each offering a unique perspective. However, the essence of all these paths remains the same: to achieve freedom not by accumulation but by unburdening, not by possession, but by surrendering to the All-Encompassing Truth. Yet, how often do popular religious practices remain rooted in this Luminous core? The teachings of great Spiritual pioneers, born of profound inner realisations, are obscured by dense layers of doctrines, dogmas, and ritualistic forms, leaving their essential Spirit hidden beneath the surface. True Religion does not reside in outer forms but in Inner Awakening, in the Soul's ascent towards its Divine origin.

## Living a Spiritual Life

Spiritual values reshape the individual's very being, remoulding it into the image of the Divine. They are not meant for fleeting happiness or escape from difficulty but for unveiling one's highest Truth.

The Universe must not be viewed as a mere machine, but as a Temple of the Infinite—a sacred space reflecting boundless Divine power. What appears as material is, in reality, a concentrated expression of God's Infinite Potential. Life, then, is a Sacred pilgrimage, with the human Soul as its deepest sanctuary.

Seen through the Soul's lens, the world appears suffused with a Divine affinity that intertwines every element—a mystical unity between objects, events, individuals, and all existence.

One discerns the Eternal rhythms in the rustle of leaves, the flow of brooks, and sermons of Truth inscribed in stones and stars. To live the high ideal of Spiritual life—especially amidst the ceaseless demands of worldly existence—is to tread a path as narrow and perilous as a *razor's edge.* As a householder, the seeker faces manifold challenges, where materialism and dogmatism, like twin spectres, threaten to undermine the Spirit's resolve. Materialism denies the Divine and glorifies the ephemeral; dogmatism veils the Infinite with a finite substitute, offering seductive shortcuts that ultimately betray the Soul's true quest.

These forces work subtly yet insidiously, casting doubts, ridiculing Faith, and magnifying difficulties to dissuade the seeker. But for every fall, the aspirant must rise with renewed vigour, for each victory over temptation builds the strength to face mightier battles. The Spiritual Journey demands Faith, endurance, and an unwavering alignment of the will with the Divine Purpose.

## The Torchbearer

The seeker is called to become a Luminous beacon, like a solitary keeper of a lighthouse amidst storm and darkness. Amidst turbulence and desolation, he ascends to kindle the flame that guides others lost in the vast seas of existence. Let us strive to be such a Torchbearer—dispelling ignorance, kindling hope, and lighting the way for weary Souls adrift upon the ocean of life. Through Faith, perseverance, and surrender, may we rise to illuminate the path to the Infinite, becoming not merely seekers but instruments of the Divine Will.

# CHAPTER 5

# Theism vs Atheism

When Buddhism and Jainism, voicing the discontent of millions against the prevailing socio-religious order, swept across India with vigour, Hindu scholars and leaders grew deeply unsettled. To preserve the continuity of the Vedic tradition, they devised the categories of *Astika* and *Nastika* to suit their purpose. According to their verdict, an *Astika*, Theist, is the one who affirms the infallible authority of the Vedas, while a *Nastika*, Atheist, is the one who doubts or rejects it.

The intention was evidently to banish Buddhism and Jainism, both of which defied Vedic authority. Yet, this definition never took root among the people. In common understanding, unchanged even today, an *Astika* is simply one who believes in God, and a *Nastika* one who does not.

## The Six Schools: *Shad-darsanas*

Hindu philosophical thought was eventually codified and systematised into six classical schools: Kapila's *Sankhya Sastra*, Kanada's *Visheshika Sastra*, Patanjali's *Yoga Sastra*, Gotama's *Nyaya Sastra*, Jaimini's *Purva Mimamsa*, and Vyasa's *Uttara Mimamsa*, also called *Vedanta Mimamsa* or *Sariraka Mimamsa*. While united in their reverence for the Vedas, these schools diverged in their views of God—some omitting Him altogether, others granting only a nominal role.

These six systems of philosophy are known as *Shad-darsanas*. These schools have wide disagreement regarding the nature and relationship of the ultimate Truth of existence with the individual Soul or *Prakriti.* However, the Immortality of the human Soul, its liberation, the Law of *Karma,* and Vedic authority are the cornerstones of these schools of thought. Prof. Max Müller described these as '*eternal riddles posed by a highly gifted race to Humanity*'.

While earlier schools varied in their treatment of Divinity, only the *Vedanta Mimamsa* positively, clearly, and emphatically asserts the existence of God. The learned believed that a Godless religion could not gain popularity, so they allowed people to believe in God.

After prolonged discussions in many Hindu Maha Sabha meetings, the leaders defined Hinduism as *any religion born in India.* This was before the country was partitioned. If this definition must be accepted, the *Charvaka* religion, which is characterised by materialism that rejects the idea of an afterlife, the Soul, the Immortality of the Self, and the sanctity of the Vedas, must also be considered a part of Hinduism. The definition, however, reflected less a quest for Truth than a desire to exclude their adversaries, Islam and Christianity.

In modern India, the reform movement came to be known as "Theism," a name chosen to suggest universality and freedom from sectarian confines. Theism rejected no tradition outright, yet bound itself to none. It accepted no scripture as final, yet reverenced all scriptures and prophets. Such an outlook—evolved, universal, and progressive—could not be tied to any denomination, and thus was called simply *Theism.*

Even when varying connotations are set aside, the fundamental distinction between Theism and Atheism still warrants examination, as all views and ways of life can broadly be classified under one or the other. It is equally necessary to consider the many schools of thought that arise within each.

## Theism or Atheism? A *Sadhak's* Dilemma

Atheism holds that this life is the ultimate reality and that there is nothing higher or beyond it. For Atheists, life is to be enjoyed to the fullest; whatever aids enjoyment is good, whatever hinders it is evil. While knowledge, intelligence, and talent are tools for enjoying this life, virtues like morality, honesty and even Faith in God or gods are beneficial only if they bring worldly success and gratification of one's ego.

In contrast, Theism posits a Truth, a principle, a consciousness higher than this life. Theists consider life not as the goal but a stage, an instrument, an opportunity to realise that Truth. If Truth can be called God, the realisation of that Truth—or God—is life's aim, goal, and purpose. The difference is fundamental: for Atheism, life is the end; for Theism, life is the means to an End beyond itself.

If life is accepted as a means toward a higher aim, then pleasure and pain, success and failure, honour and humiliation lose their absolute value. They no longer define us. Moreover, from a higher Divine perspective, these experiences become vehicles—events that refine the Soul, challenge the ego, and illuminate the deeper Truth within. In this light, ethical and Spiritual values assume supreme importance. Truthfulness, Love, and the awareness of God's Presence are not just desirable—they are essential, for they nourish the Soul in its journey toward the Eternal.

A *Sadhak* encounters countless distractions and dissuasions along his path. Atheistic tendencies surreptitiously rise within him, whispering temptations and offering the cunning arguments of the devil himself, urging him to abandon his Spiritual quest. Questions press upon him—'*What is the value of honesty, truthfulness, integrity, or arduous meditation and prayer in today's fast-paced world?*' His materialistic side insists that only those who are firmly grounded, practical, and shrewd can succeed and be happy. It counsels a so-called reality check—rejecting ideals that do not yield tangible gain, and embracing the laws of material success.

To such a view, nothing seems more foolish than forgoing the pleasures of this life in pursuit of peace or happiness in an *imaginary* Eternal life after death. In this reasoning, lofty concepts and austere practices appear worthless in a world so advanced.

However, at the heart of the *Sadhak's* struggle lies a choice—not merely between belief and disbelief, but between fleeting fulfilment and enduring meaning.

## The Victory of Atheism

Atheism has influenced religions both directly and indirectly, often masquerading as a form of Religion. Many popular religious beliefs and practices, when analysed, reveal traces of Atheism, like rituals performed without true Faith that reduce Religion to mere social custom or mockery. Atheism attacks Theism in two ways—direct Atheism denies God outright, while indirect Atheism presents a false or distorted concept of Him. The latter is more dangerous. Atheism's most insidious victory lies not in the denial of God but in corrupting the very idea of Him.

False concepts of Divinity breed bigotry, sectarianism, fanaticism, and hatred—atrocities committed in the name of God. Such distortion, more than denial, is Atheism's greatest victory.

## Essence of Sacrifice and Virtue

Falsehood and hypocrisy are not restricted to Religion and the idea of God. They seep deeply into certain other artificially glorified concepts. However, the Truth lies beyond appearances and even in the depths of falsehood. Take, for instance, the idea of sacrifice. People from all schools of thought glorify 'sacrifice'—whether a mother's sacrifice for her child or a patriot's sacrifice for the motherland.

But the true essence of sacrifice can be understood only from a higher perspective of this Universe. The seed sacrifices itself to become a tree, infancy sacrifices for babyhood, babyhood for boyhood, boyhood for youth, and youth for manhood. Sacrifice is the Law of life and growth—surrendering a smaller value for a greater one. Hence, when we glorify life-sacrifice, we imply that there is something more precious than life itself.

Whatever helps one to realise the Truth is a virtue, and whatever hides the Truth or hinders its realisation is evil. Virtue upholds human dignity and decency—life in Spirit, life in God, life in Eternity. Virtue brings one nearer to reality and the reality of all existence. The value of virtue lies in the moral satisfaction it brings rather than any external rewards or benefits. Admiring virtue only when it aligns with our interests amounts to hypocrisy. As the Roman orator and philosopher, Cicero, wisely noted, *"Virtue is its own reward."*

## *Chaturvidha Purshardha Sadhana*

For a right living, our ancients prescribed a formula known as *Chaturvidha Purshardha Sadhana*: *Dharma*, *Artha*, *Kama*, *Moksha*.

*Dharma* is ethical righteousness necessary for a dignified life and social order. *Artha*, wealth in all its nobler forms, is essential to living and expressing the great truths of life. *Kama* encompasses a wide range of desires that are essential for the dynamism of life. *Moksha* is liberation from the bondage of ignorance and weakness. It is the destiny of the Soul.

The genius of this scheme lies in its balance: *Artha* and *Kama* are to be guided by *Dharma* and oriented toward *Moksha*. Without this higher alignment, wealth and desire degenerate into ends in themselves, leading to distortion.

Human progress, though radiant in its outer achievements, has begun to take a grotesque turn. In the haste to win the race of education and career, many overlook the deeper foundations of life. The treasures of the Spirit—truthfulness, compassion, reverence—are often neglected, sometimes even discouraged, as though they were hindrances to worldly success.

Yet no accomplishment can replace the quiet strength that comes from an inner anchoring in noble values. It is this inner wealth, more than material inheritance, that endures across generations. To nurture a home where generosity of heart, clarity of thought, and reverence for the Eternal are cherished is to leave behind a legacy far greater than possessions. This legacy illumines the path of those who come after us.

*Home is the most fundamental of all human institutions.* While an individual is valued for his accomplishments and usefulness, his intrinsic value is recognised at *home,* where he was born and brought up. This is the place where great lessons of life and Divine qualities are first learned.

*A noble Soul, born in a humble home, can illuminate the whole world.—Anonymous.*

## CHAPTER 6

# Essence of Monotheism

In an age marked by Spiritual fragmentation and institutional rigidity on one hand, and the proliferation of self-proclaimed godmen with unconventional concepts and dogmas on the other, the yearning for a unifying, liberating Truth grows more insistent. It is into this atmosphere of both confusion and longing that Monotheism steps forward, offering perhaps the most holistic remedy—one that speaks directly to both inner liberation and collective healing.

Although God pervades throughout time and space, He is not confined to a particular moment, whether it be a second, a minute, an hour, a day, a week, a month, a year, or even a century. Nor is He bound to any single particle of matter or object. He is the invisible Spirit dwelling within all things visible, the formless essence within forms, the personal Presence in the impersonal, and the Silent Law that directs all transitions from cause to consequence.

God is the sound hidden in the ether, the meaning folded in the sound, the light that waits in the lamp, the vision that awakens the eye, the fire asleep in the wood, the song that breathes through the flute, the nectar secreted in the flower, and the Spirit ensouled in the body.

God must be conceived by the Mind, felt by the Heart, and experienced by the Soul. As the *Bhagavad Gita* says, *"He shines through things. But He is not those things."*

If we perceive God as the only All-perfect Being, we must accept that there cannot be more than one All-perfect Being. No object, person, or scripture can be equated with Him. The Universe of time and space is within God. His revelation and activity are not confined to any particular place or period. Geographical boundaries cannot limit our affinity or reverence for Him. Even during adulations or ceremonies, we must not visualise God as residing at a specific point in space-time. By perceiving Him as the Eternal, we come to understand that He is present everywhere, in everything, and at all times—past, present, and future.

## Our Inner Guides

Within every human heart resides a spark of the Divine—a seed of Infinite Potential awaiting its awakening. Conscience and Reason serve as inner guides, illuminating man's path toward Self-Realisation. Truth, wherever found, is to be embraced with humility, for each insight is a fragment of the Eternal Whole. Nevertheless, one also retains the right to reject that which does not resonate with personal Conscience or Reason. This right of Spiritual discernment lies at the heart of Monotheistic self-determination, guiding seekers on a path of conscious alignment with Truth. Monotheistic Faith thus becomes a chosen Truth—not an imposed doctrine—but one deepened through Communion and Worship, making the Spiritual journey dynamic and fruitful.

This Inner Light must shape outer life. The Spiritual ideal is Universal in its essence, yet profoundly human in its expression. It transcends divisions, affirming the oneness of God, the Unity of Humanity, and the harmony of Existence.

A true Monotheist does not consider himself as belonging to any sect. He thinks of every sect seeking Spiritual life as his own. His Spiritual sustenance is through Prayer, Adoration, and Meditation. He reverently performs all his daily activities and considers everything around him Sacred.

The heart of the Monotheistic creed lies not in a fixed set of doctrines but in a way of life that responds spiritually to the complexities of human experience. This creed embodies a mindset that yearns for limitless development and freedom. At its core, it is Spiritual and Universal in nature.

Monotheism is an integral feature of every major theistic tradition, including Hinduism, Buddhism, Christianity, Islam, Zoroastrianism, and Sikhism. However, it transcends the popular forms of these religions, aligning with the Spiritual essence found within each.

Thoughtful individuals across all religions have advocated for pure theism, condemning false religion regardless of its label. The essence of Monotheistic creeds can be understood by different names or no name at all. Several names may inspire people, but all Monotheistic believers find a place within a common Spiritual framework regardless of religious denomination.

Pandit Sivanath Sastry, a visionary leader, emphasised that a seeker of pure Monotheism must break away from religions with aberrant or false views of Monotheism and join the caravan of like-minded Spiritual travellers. With profound ideas and holistic ideals about Monotheism, they can meet, discuss, and pray together to the only Formless, Omnipresent Creator. They may refer to their congregation as a *Prarthana Samaj, Mukti Samaj*, or any other name they prefer. The modes of Worship and forms of rituals and domestic ceremonies may vary. However, if the fundamental tenets—Immortality of the *Soul*, direct Spiritual Worship, the Universality of Revelation, and the Brotherhood of Man—are upheld, they will embody the essence of Monotheistic Faith. The colour and complexion of this Faith need not and should not be uniform across all contexts. Keshub Chandra Sen, a Spiritual luminary, echoed this sentiment, emphasising that divergence arises from local, racial, and traditional differences.

Movements like Unitarianism in Christianity, Sufism, Bahaism, and Islam are often seen as counterparts to Monotheistic creeds like Brahmo Samaj, sharing an affinity. Emphasis on religious denomination and tradition can lead to sectarianism, which opposes theistic and universal principles.

Flexibility and the capacity for variation in expression and form preserve the Spirit within. The ability to adapt is a testament to the *vitality* that enriches the *Soul.*

## Loyalty to Truth and God

Monotheists should be more loyal to Truth and God than to institutions and names. We must appreciate that such institutions are starting points, not destinations. We should accept all individuals worldwide who think rightly, act boldly and nobly, regardless of their religious denomination.

Reducing Monotheism to a religious sect or community, emphasising a particular name and form, and creating a new caste would inflict a fatal blow on the Universal and unifying Spirit of Monotheistic Faith.

Is an organisation unnecessary, then? Is initiation wrong? Undoubtedly, an organisation is necessary, and initiation has its unique significance. It is invaluable for collective worship and work. It unites liberal and progressive thinkers of all theistic paths, fosters fraternity, provides a congenial atmosphere for moral and Spiritual growth, and facilitates the exchange of ideas and experiences. It should be a nurturing centre for religious life, open to all seekers irrespective of religious biases. It should celebrate meaningful festivals of all religions from a theistic perspective.

However, it is not right to overemphasise an organisation's name, feel superior for being a member of that organisation, and think of others as inferior. This attitude fosters vanity and religious ego, leading to contempt, self-justification, and a propensity for retaliation. Thus, it does a great disservice to the original aspiration to establish a holistic Monotheistic Faith.

The power of Monotheistic Faith shines brightest when its principles are presented without attachment to name. However, people who normally hesitate when a new name is mentioned will often view Monotheism, sans a label, with greater suspicion. While this prejudice is unjustifiable, it cannot be ignored. What ultimately matters is not the designation but the essence: how faithfully its followers embody integrity, morality, spirituality, and service to the common good. If these ideals are lived with sincerity, they will speak more convincingly than any name or absence of name, calling each adherent to a deep and honest self-examination.

## Initiation to Monotheism

To mark the breakaway of a seeker from inherited practices and embrace a new and liberated Spiritual path, an initiation ceremony is crucial. This ceremony, which explains the reasons for the new path, not only fosters determination but also brings a sense of liberation to the weary Soul. It is essential to recognise that such an initiation is not a religious conversion but rather an entry into a Spiritual culture akin to culturally accepted ceremonies, such as *Aksharabhyasa* (Ceremonial initiation of a child to read and write), *Upanayana Samskara* (Ceremonial initiation for boys to start Vedic education), *or Dwijatva* (Ceremonial declaration of a child born again into knowledge and duty).

Keshub Chandra Sen references this in the fourth chapter of his Spiritual Autobiography, the *Jeevan Veda.* Rabindranath Tagore discusses this concept as a second birth in his book, *Personality.*

Initiation involves a declaration of Faith in Monotheism, monolatry, and Universal theism, as well as a commitment to live by these principles. This public declaration has a moral impact, solidifying wavering beliefs into steadfast loyalty. To honour its solemnity and guard against flippancy, initiation must be regarded as a formal and Sacred occasion. The act of initiation serves to promote and declare True Religion openly. The initiation day is a significant event and a powerful reminder in times of crisis. *Spiritual initiation, while external in form, is inwardly a reaffirmation—a breaking of inherited patterns and an embracing of inner freedom.*

## Rationalism and Spiritual Practice

In the context of reform movements, Monotheistic Faiths embody what Sri Aurobindo described as a strong dose of *Religious Rationalism.* This rationalism is not just a philosophical stance but a necessary tool in Spiritual practice. An excessive focus on rationalism can result in superficial Spirituality, while neglecting rationalism can lead to dogmatism, superstition, reliance on external authority, and a tendency to be drawn to personality cults—all of which are denounced by Monotheistic Faiths. Therefore, Monotheistic believers must practice constant vigilance and self-examination as they lead their holistic Spiritual lives. This balance between *Pure Reason* and *Heartfelt Devotion* is not easily maintained. It requires alertness, humility, and genuine self-reflection. As the *Upanishads* aptly put it, Spiritual practice is akin to *walking on the edge of a razor blade.*

# CHAPTER 7

# Brahma Stotram

ॐ नमस्ते सतेते जगत्कारणाय।
नमस्ते चिते सर्वलोकाश्रयाय॥
नमोऽद्वैततत्त्वाय मुक्तिप्रदाय।
नमो ब्रह्मणे व्यापिने शाश्वताय॥

*Salutations to Thee, O Truth—Source of the Universe; To Consciousness, the refuge of all Worlds;*
*To the Non-dual Reality, the giver of Liberation; To Brahman, the All-Pervading and Eternal.*

त्वमेकं शरण्यं त्वमेकं वरेण्यं|
त्वमेकं जगत्पालकं स्वप्रकाशम्||
त्वमेकं जगत्कर्तृ, पातृ प्रहर्तृ,
त्वमेकं परं निश्चलं निर्विकल्पम्||

*Thou alone art the refuge, the Supreme object of Reverence; Thou alone art the Protector of the World, Self-Luminous;*
*Thou alone art the Creator, Sustainer, and Dissolver; Thou art the Supreme, Unchanging, beyond all Dualities.*

भयानामभयं, भीषणं भीषणानाम्।
गतिः प्राणिनां, पावनं पावनानाम्॥
महोच्चैःपदानाम् नियन्त्रुत्वम् एकम्,
परेषाम् परं रक्षणं रक्षणानाम्॥

*Thou art Fearlessness amidst fear, the Terror of terrors; The Goal of all beings, the Purifier of the pure;*
*The sole Controller of those in Exalted States; The Supreme Protector of all protectors.*

वयं त्वाम् स्मरामो, वयं त्वाम् भजामो।
वयं त्वाम् जगत्साक्षिरूपम् नमामः॥
सदेकम् निदानम् निरालम्बम् ईशम्,
भवाम्बोधिपोतम् शरण्यम् व्रजामः॥

*We remember Thee, we worship Thee; We bow to Thee, the Witness of the World;*

*Thou art the Eternal Source, the unsupported Lord; We seek refuge in Thee, the boat across the ocean of Becoming.*

The foregoing verses, known as the *Brahma Stotram,* praise the God of *Upanishadic* thought—distinct from the conceptions found in the *Puranas.* Originally drawn from the *Mahanirvana Tantra,* this hymn transcends sectarian boundaries, carrying the essence of *Advaitic* philosophy, later refined by Devendranath Tagore to reflect a more universal resonance.

Unlike *Puranic* conceptions that often depict Divinity through form, action, and narrative, this hymn speaks of God in His Transcendental Formlessness—an understanding central to *Upanishadic* Wisdom.

Therefore, this *stotra* does not describe God's physical form, decorations, or weapons; nor does it elaborate on Divine acts of protection and dissolution. Its content is far deeper, more integral, and spiritually enriching. In this sense, it becomes not merely a hymn of praise but also a philosophical exposition, unveiling God's Nature and His relation to the Universe.

## God and His Cosmic Drama

The first stanza suggests the *Cosmic Drama* of the Universe, encompassing four acts. Each of the four lines contains dual concepts: God as *Sat*—the Existence and Cause of the Universe; God as *Chit*—Self-Luminous and the refuge of all beings; God as the One who grants *Salvation*; and God as Transcendent and Eternal. These verses unveil both God's *Inherent Nature* and His relation to the Universe.

God is not only Existence but also the Cause of all that exists. He is not one among many things; He is the Source of everything. He is Existence itself—gross or subtle, animate or inanimate, on any plane at any time. There is no cause for His Being, for all causes derive from Him. He is the First Cause—not first in time or space, but foundational, as nothing exists without Him. Just as a shadow cannot exist without substance, so too can nothing exist apart from Him.

God is not an architect removed from His creation, nor a craftsman who steps away after fashioning His work. He is the Ever-Present Reality—woven into the fabric of Existence, animating every motion, every breath. It is His Presence that sustains the orbits of planets, the flutter of eyelids, the silent rhythms of respiration and blood.

God is *Chit—Self-Existent, Self-Luminous.* As the Cause of all that exists, He is the Light of all lights. The Universe shines in His Light—nothing can shine independently. From the glow of a distant star to the flicker of a candle, no radiance exists apart from Him.

Yet His Light is more than physical. It is the inner Illumination of Wisdom, Memory, Intuition, and the Soul's awakening.

*'Memory, Knowledge, even Forgetfulness are possible because of Me,'* declares *Srikrishna.*

God is intimately involved with the Universe and every creature, guiding and guarding each person. Nothing transpires outside His Awareness. We must learn to feel safe and secure in Him and seek His Guidance at every step.

God is the Unifier and the giver of Salvation. Salvation lies in realising His Unity. In Him, the Unifier, all confusions are cleared, contradictions reconciled, and mysteries revealed. Light and Darkness, Life and Death, Good and Evil are all possible because He is the Root of all. In one, He is more revealed; in another, more concealed. He is not merely a unit among many—He is Unity itself: common to all, connecting all, including all, and surpassing all.

## Salvation, Liberation and Unity

Salvation is the Realisation of the essential Unity of all Existence—the dissolving of separation and the awakening to Wholeness. Yet what holds us back from this Truth? The *ego*, with its narrow grasp on identity, and its *illusion of division*. The Divinity within us is constantly trying to liberate us from the limits of the perishable, from the bounds of the localised Self—the ego. *Ego* may pretend to be the Soul, but it is not so. At best, the ego is its shadow. The ego separates us from others, while the Soul unites us with all. Once this pretence is realised, the Soul is naturally released in its full glory and merges into the indivisible rhythm of Existence.

*Mukti* is not merely freedom from the pleasures of sensuousness or selfish desires, but the Joy that springs from renouncing egoism. It is the Divine fulfilment every aspirant yearns to attain. It is the attunement of the Self with the rhythm of Nature and Universal Life—a descent beneath the superficial Self into deeper realms of Being.

This quest for *Unity* is not only Spiritual but also the hidden impulse behind all human knowledge. The work of a physicist is fulfilled in the discovery of a single law or force from which all laws and forces derive; the chemist's work reaches completion upon finding out that one element from which all chemicals arise; the botanist's work concludes upon finding that one herb from which the entire vegetable kingdom has grown. Thus, every branch of knowledge aims to discover the one Source of all.

All philosophy is an intellectual attempt to explain the relation of the *One* and the *many*. The final mystery and ultimate meaning lie in the fundamental *Unity* of all Existence.

*True wisdom lies in seeing through illusion to perceive the Unity that connects all things beneath outward distinctions.*

## Proximity to God

Nearness to God is not understood in terms of time or space, but rather in terms of growing in nature that is similar to the Divine. To move closer to God is not to shift in location—it is to expand in Consciousness, to grow into a Nature that reflects His Boundlessness. Nor is this nearness conditioned by causation; it is timeless, arising from the transformation of nature.

The Unity of God realised by the *Sadhak* encompasses and transcends all particulars and is Eternal. *Namo Brahmane Vyapine Saaswataaya.*

Existence unfolds in four acts—an emergence from undifferentiation, a journey through multiplicity, a homecoming to Unity, and an Eternal continuation of this *Cosmic Rhythm.* Creation is the process by which the *One* becomes many while maintaining its *Oneness.*

The progression of each entity at its own pace and temperament constitutes the second stage, as they move through various experiences. After a time, each entity realises its final meaning and ultimate Destiny by experiencing harmony with the All. This is the third stage. Recognising the Eternity of this Harmony is the fourth stage.

The remaining three stanzas reiterate with force God's Unity, Glory, Power, Purity, and Majesty. His power is meant to uplift us to His level. The word *'Ekam'* occurs six times in the three stanzas, infusing confidence that He deserves to be depended upon as the True Well-Wisher forever—*Gatih Praninaam.* The verses should be chanted with enthusiasm and Devotion. This recurring invocation is not a mechanical reiteration—it is a living call to trust, a reaffirmation that in Divine Oneness lies the Soul's *Ultimate Refuge.*

# CHAPTER 8

# The Upanishadic Prayer

1

एना अहं नामृतास्याम् ।
किमहं तेन कुर्याम् ।

2

असतो मा सद्गमय ।
तमसो मा ज्योतिर्गमय ।
मृत्योर्मामृतं गमय ॥

3

अविरावीर् मा एधि ।

4

रुद्र! यत्ते दक्षिणं मुखम् ।
तेन मां पाहि नित्यम् ॥

This Prayer comprises four parts. The first part is from one section of the *Brihadaranyaka Upanishad*, the second draws from a different portion of the same *Upanishad*, the third part is from the *Aitareya Upanishad*, and the last part is from the *Svetasvatara Upanishad*. Together, these verses express the loftiest Spiritual aspirations of the human Soul, reflecting humanity's Eternal hopes, dreams, struggles, and endeavours toward Self-Discovery and Transcendence.

Although it may seem simple, the richness and sublimity of its thought are boundless, making it relevant at all stages and phases of the Soul's Journey.

*Ena aham naamritasyaam* ।
*Kim aham tena kuryaam* ।

The Prayer suggests Life's Aim and Purpose, the Soul's highest Destiny, and the meaning of Existence in its first line. This line emphasises the aspirations of the human Soul and conveys the vanity of things that do not help realise the *Soul's* Immortal Nature.

It asks, '*What shall I do with things that do not give me Immortality?*'

## From the Unreal to the Real

*Asato maa Sadgamaya* ।

*Lead me from the Unreal to the Real.* This is the primal cry of the human Soul, for man is constantly surrounded by the appearance of things, mistaking shadow for substance and the transient for the enduring.

The world dazzles with glitter, yet much of what it offers is only a surface play—forms that fade, pleasures that wither, promises that betray.

The seers of the *Upanishads* discerned that this veil of unreality, which we call *Maya*, is not sheer falsehood but a partial truth—a distortion of the Eternal. The *Unreal* is not non-existent; it is the half-seen, the broken fragment, the seeming, when taken as the Whole.

To cling to it as final is to wander in darkness. To rise beyond it is to behold the *Sat*, the Reality which alone endures.

The Prayer is thus a call to discrimination: to awaken the Inner Eye that distinguishes between the passing and the

Permanent, between the glitter of semblance and the radiance of Truth. The Soul does not merely yearn to escape illusion; it yearns to be established in that which *is*—the Sat, the Foundation of all Existence, the Eternal substratum of all forms and movements.

When the seeker utters *Asato maa sadgamaya*, he asks not only for guidance but for transformation: that his being may be weaned away from the lures of appearance and rooted in the Reality which is God, Self, and Truth.

*It is the first rung of the ladder of Immortality, without which no ascent is possible.*

## Truth and the Transience of Life

Truth is that which exists in its own right—Self-Luminous, independent, not borrowed from anything else. By contrast, all else bears the mark of transience: momentary, perishable, ever subject to change.

Every Soul arrives with this ingrained *Knowledge*. It knows that everything in the world is continually changing and disappearing, just like shifting clouds that take on the shapes of a lion, a rabbit, a tree, or an old woman, only to dissolve again. *Change alone is changeless.* Things perish, events change, and values and relationships transform. The body changes, the Mind changes, and the entire life changes. Therefore, the *Sadhak* says:

*'Let me not have glamour for things swallowed by time and conditions. Let my Soul be attached forever to things and Values that are enduring. Let Truth be dearer to me than all things put together.'*

Everything finite suggests the Infinite. So, our attachment to things should not be for themselves but only as revelations of the Infinite, as aids to realise the Permanent. This truth is beautifully expressed in the Upanishadic dictum:

*Ajaayamano Bahudhah Vijayate - 'That which has no birth is born again and again in many forms.'*

To that Eternal, the seeker turns with a heart full of devotion and sings—

*'Thou art our Mother and Father. Thou art our Guru and Guide. Thou art our Kith and Kin. Thou art our Wealth and Wisdom. Thou art our All in All.'*

The Motherliness in the mother, the Protection in the father, the Enlightenment of the Guru, the Affection in kith and kin, the Wisdom, glory, and value in everything are Divine. God is not only a remote, Transcendental, Extra-Cosmic Reality, but also immanent in and through the fabric and texture of life. Thus, there is a re-evaluation of everything, within and around us.

Concepts, Values, things, and even Relations are first rejected and later re-interpreted and accepted. These re-evaluations are like previously closed windows, now flung open, revealing the boundless sky and the Self-Effulgent Sun. Unrelated to God, we stand on blind alleys. Related to God, we walk on the royal road to a magnificent world. In sensuous things, too, we should learn to sense the Supersensuous.

## Light, Darkness and Realising the One

*Tamasoma Jyotir gamaya |*

*Tamas* is *Darkness, Ignorance; Jyothi* is *Light, Knowledge.* Knowledge comes in two forms: differentiation and Unity. Differentiation of Knowledge is known as *Avidya* and *Bhedagnana.* Knowledge of Unity, realising that nothing is fundamentally different from anything else, is *Vidya, Abhedagnana.* The former, though necessary, does not reveal the most profound Truth of things. It is only through the latter, *Abhedagnana,* that one perceives the One—Unity, Harmony, the Supreme Destiny of the Soul.

The One supports the many. The many reveal the One and its Infinite Power and richness. Without the One, there are no 'many'.

Without the many, the One cannot be known. One is the substance, and many are its expressions.

Here is how a seeker comprehends this idea. Love is the One; its manifestations are many. Truth is One; its aspects, faces, and facets are many. Man is one, and his relations are many. The One is the cause, and many are the consequences. *God is One in Being, manifold in Becoming—the Multiple One.*

In Creation, the multitude often obscures the Unity behind it. The essence of Existence is Unity, hidden beneath the layers of diversity, discord, and division. Understanding this concept involves recognising that these surface differences are merely varied expressions of the same underlying Truth.

Enlightenment comes with the Realisation that what appears as many, and even as opposites, are all manifestations of a singular Reality. One must strive to see beyond the Multiplicity and not be misled by the Diversity of forms. True understanding involves recognising that each aspect of Creation uniquely expresses the same fundamental Truth.

When this Unity is perceived, the differences do not disappear; instead, they harmonise. Conflicts transform into concord, and disparate elements work together seamlessly, like petals forming a flower or fingers forming a hand. Each distinct part reveals the *Unified Essence* in its unique way, creating a Harmonious existence.

The concept of Oneness is what gives meaning to the multiplicity of Existence. Just as fingers combine to form a grip, eyes converge to provide sight, and ears synchronise to hear, all elements of Creation converge to reveal a unified whole. This Unity liberates each element from isolation and connects it to a harmonious whole.

Understanding this Unity's Omnipresent and All-Transcendent Nature involves recognising that every object and event is interconnected within the vast expanse of space and time.

This Realisation of Oneness is the essence of Harmony and the foundation of a coherent, Interconnected Existence.

## From Death to Immortality

*Mrityormaa amrutamgamaya* I

This powerful Prayer is expressed by a seeker who longs to be guided from the realm of death to Eternal Life, from fear and sorrow to the Wisdom that demonstrates that nothing truly Sacred or Divine is ever truly destroyed. The seeker fervently asks to be guided from death-like separation from the Divine towards an Eternal Union with It. It is a plea to be drawn away from attachment to the material and towards a deeper connection with the spirit.

The Prayer continues with a heartfelt request for the discernment to distinguish between form and substance, shadow and Reality, body and Soul, and the perishable from the Imperishable. The seeker longs for the awakening of insight to see the many forms of the same substance and to recognise the same Essence in various manifestations. Acknowledging that the Body, Life, and Mind are nothing but temporary vehicles for the Soul's Journey, the seeker passionately affirms their True, Eternal Nature.

This intense aspiration reflects a deep desire for Spiritual clarity, the understanding of Eternal Truths, and the Realisation of the Timeless Essence that connects all of Existence.

When a dear one dies, sorrow wells up from the silent spaces of love, where Presence once lived and now only memory lingers. We do not grieve the body, but the breath, the glance, the voice that made life feel whole. The ache is not for what is gone, but for what once touched us so deeply that we cannot imagine being untouched. In that hollow silence, we are comforted by a *Divine Spark*—embedded in our unconscious like an *Eternal Memory*—

rising now to our rescue, reminding us that the Soul is never truly lost.

The Prayer that follows becomes a doorway through grief into the atrium of the Eternal. It does not seek to erase sorrow, but to sanctify it—and gently reveal what truly endures. For in the stillness beyond loss, the Soul hears a deeper call—not for what was taken, but for what truly is.

## Immortality of the Soul

Immortality is the intrinsic quality of the human Soul. If God is Eternal, man, the child of God, is Eternal, too. If *Paramathman* is Immortal, the *Jeevathman,* an emanation of *Paramathman,* is Immortal.

According to the *Upanishadic* seers, Immortality is not the continuation of bodily existence, but a Transcendence of the Law of causation and the attainment of the highest form of Spiritual freedom. From this exalted state, the Liberated Soul may either choose to return to earthly life to assist other Souls in their ascent or remain in the freedom of Spiritual Liberation.

The seeker ardently prays for Enlightenment to realise his True Self, which reflects the Divine Nature, and to distinguish it from his superficial Self. He yearns for Divine Guidance to reach a state of Eternal Unity with the Divine Essence.

This aspiration, known as '*atma-anatma viveka*', embodies *Spiritual Wisdom* that discerns the true Self from the not-self, the essence of 'me' from what is not 'me'. The seeker does not pray for an indefinite extension of the present life nor the perpetuation of the current state in any form, be it animal, plant, or even something superhuman. Instead, the seeker yearns for a kind of Immortality revealed in the *Upanishads*: not the continuation of body or Mind, but the Realisation of the Spirit—Timeless, Formless, and Liberated.

In the initial stages of the seeker's path, the Knowledge of Differentiation — *bhedagnana* — serves a vital purpose. It awakens discernment between the Transient and the Eternal, the Perishable and the Imperishable. Through this insight, the seeker learns detachment from the ephemeral and prepares the inner being for higher Realisation. Yet detachment alone does not complete the Journey. It is through the Luminous Knowledge of Oneness — *abhedagnana*—that the seeker transcends duality and awakens to the glory of the All-Pervading, All-Penetrating Universal Spirit. Thus, the conquest of death is not merely in withdrawal, but in identification with the Eternal.

This union with the Universal Spirit signifies the attainment of Immortality. Thus, conquering death and achieving Immortality are two interconnected phases of the same Spiritual Journey.

## A Plea for Divine Revelation

*Aviraaviram aedhi* I

*"Reveal Thyself to me."* This is the plea of seekers who acknowledge that the Divine had always provided for their needs even before they were aware of them. However, the devotees feel a deep yearning for the Presence of the Divine itself rather than just its gifts. They express that material blessings are insufficient without the Divine Presence and that they would find true happiness in the direct revelation of the Divine. The *Sadhak* is not content to perceive the Divine through Nature, history, or saints—for these remain intermediaries.

*"Let me not rest content with echoes of Thy Name, nor with shadows of Thy Light. Let me behold Thee—not in symbol, but in silence, not in promise, but in Presence."* — From a seeker's Prayer.

The Splendour of Creation dazzles the eye and fills the heart with wonder, yet it is this very Splendour that veils the timeless Reality behind it. The Eternal hides, not in Darkness, but in

Brilliance—covered by its own radiance, concealed by the beauty of its manifestation. Behind the Brilliance lies the One, and the Soul longs to behold it as its own deepest Being.

## From Awe to Ascent

*Rudra! Yette dakshanam mukham I Tena maam pahi nityam II*

*"O Rudra, reveal Thy Peaceful Countenance and protect me forever with Thy immediate Presence and direct Contact."*- This is a poignant appeal of the seeker, overwhelmed by the awe of the Divine.

When Lord Krishna unveiled His Universal Form before Arjuna, the warrior too was unable to endure its Splendour and Terror. Trembling, he confessed—*"Dhritim na vindami samanche Vishno"—I cannot maintain my composure, O Vishnu. Reveal once more Thy form of Peace."*

The idea in the *Svetasvatara Upanishad* thus finds its echo in the *Bhagavad Gita*: man, in his finite being, yearns not merely for the vision of Divine Power but for the solace of Divine Peace.

It was the Spiritual genius of Maharshi Devendranath Tagore to gather luminous gems of Wisdom from four scattered passages across three Upanishads and weave them into one seamless Prayer. In it, we witness a clear progression of aspiration:

*"What shall I do with that which does not grant Immortality?*
*Let Truth be dearer to me than all else.*
*Grant me the Knowledge of Unity.*
*Let me not identify with what is perishable.*
*My rest and my joy are in Thee, and Thee alone."*

This gradual ascent of appeal, rising from renunciation of the transient to the embrace of the Eternal, makes the Prayer a veritable ladder to Immortality.

Yet one must remember, when we utter this Prayer, it must be with the utmost sincerity. To invoke such a Prayer is to summon its fulfilment; we must be willing to accept, with cheerfulness, the consequences that follow if it is truly granted.

This profound Prayer, preserved in the *Upanishads,* is rarely offered in Hindu homes or temples, yet, distilled and arranged by Maharshi Devendranath Tagore, it remains not merely the heritage of a single community, but a gift to the whole of Humankind.

## CHAPTER 9

# The Four Pillars of Spiritual Life

God can be known only through Experiential Realisation, and attaining such a sublime state requires a long, sustained inner effort grounded in an unshakable foundation. If the foundation is weak, the edifice is sure to collapse.

The four pillars of this foundation are *Peace of Mind, Prayer, Righteous Living, and Meditation.* Prayer and Righteousness purify and discipline Body and Mind, while Peace of Mind and Meditation still the waves of thought, opening the way for the awakening of the Soul.

Yet this path must be approached with care, for prematurely attempting to hasten the Soul's unity with the Divine could be harmful, as it may lead to psychic disturbance or inner imbalance. The aspirant risks becoming egoistic, insensitive to human feelings, and boastful of having risen above the pairs of opposites—*Dvandvas.*

Similarly, if the *Sadhak's* Mind is not at peace, Spiritual Experiences are unstable and have no lasting influence. His efforts would be as futile as pouring water into a pot riddled with holes.

A disturbed Mind is a hindrance to Spiritual Practice. Just as we cannot clearly see the bottom of a lake with disturbed waters, so too can we not perceive our inner being when the Mind is unsettled. Peace of Mind is not only indispensable for Realisation—it is a blessing in its own right.

The *Sadhak's* aim must be to awaken the Soul, with all its Divine qualities, naturally and patiently, and strive to submit to these qualities and seek guidance from them. These qualities will slowly, yet certainly, attain influence over his Mind, Body, and Life itself.

## Peace of Mind and Equanimity

Peace of Mind does not imply a Mind free of all thoughts and ideas, but the mastery of one's relationship with thought. It is but natural that thoughts of all kinds arise and move about in the Mind. Some are induced by outer stimuli. The aspirant must look at these thoughts with detachment, realising that he is the Witness, not the thinker, and learn to feel his separateness from them. Just as one remains unaffected and detached from stray words and comments heard in a public place, the aspirant must also remain unattached to the ebb and flow of thoughts in his Mind. He should allow only those thoughts that deserve his attention into his *inner space*, rejecting all others.

Our unwary Minds may not detect certain suggestions and prompts that sneak in and become embedded in the unconscious until they surface disguised as our own thoughts and take hold of the conscious Mind. At this point, it becomes difficult to distinguish them from our true Self.

However, it would be easier to differentiate between our *original* thoughts and *unfamiliar* ones if we are vigilant enough to spot them the moment they enter our minds. In the initial stage, it is desirable to spend some time every day in solitude to practise mental discernment. During this time, one must try to separate one's original thoughts from intrusive or unworthy thoughts.

Just as we reflexively close our eyes to prevent dust particles from entering, we must learn to retreat into our True Self when threatened by harmful thoughts. Once we are in our Inner Sanctum, the raging storm outside, with its devastation of uprooted trees and roofs blowing off, does not affect us. We become detached from any outward, challenging circumstances. This is possible when we identify ourselves with our Divine Nature and differentiate everything else from our true Self.

Equanimity grants the Soul a Divine perspective on Life's movements. It does not imply a dull indifference to virtue and vice, but the ability to remain inwardly untouched by either, while still standing with the forces of Truth, against the forces of Falsehood. It is like the surgeon who, with calm detachment, removes a part of the body to preserve the whole—an act stern in appearance, yet born of compassion and higher wisdom.

In rejecting hostile influences, the aspirant may draw upon Understanding, Will, or even Ego—yet these instruments offer only limited resistance. The most enduring form of rejection arises from within, through detachment. Just as a lotus remains detached from the droplets of water or mud on its petals, neither trying to shake them off nor absorb them, the aspirant, anchored in the Divine, allows external forces to pass without clinging or conflict. It is not through confrontation but through indifference—through the quiet refusal to react—that the Soul remains sovereign.

The aspirant may seek God's assistance, desiring Divine support and strength in his efforts. Nevertheless, he recognises that even if he were to fall, it would be in the Presence of the Divine and understands that his defeat in this struggle would not serve the Higher Purpose he is aligned with. With growing certainty, he becomes aware that while he is distinct from the *triple vehicle* of Body, Mind, and Life, he is also one with the underlying, Eternal, All-Pervading Consciousness.

The instruments of action tend to operate under the influence of a Lower Nature, continuing their habitual tendencies without reference to the Higher Will. An implicit fear arises that resisting these tendencies would render Life inert, deprived of vitality, spontaneity, and joy. In such a state, the *Purusha*—the Witnessing

Self—is overlooked as the True Governor of action. Instead, these faculties often remain aligned with the egos shaped by the three *Gunas*: *Sattva*, *Rajas*, and *Tamas*. At times, the instruments may seem to act in accordance with the *Purusha*, but this alignment is often illusory. The witnessing Self is detached even in such instances. It neither accepts nor rejects the workings of the three *Gunas*. It is upon the aspirant to see through their actions with detachment and thus rise in harmony with the *Purusha*.

## Faith, Transformation, and Moment of Grace

As the *Sadhak* progresses on his Spiritual journey, he often finds himself in a state where the results of his efforts seem out of reach. When the outcomes are not immediately apparent, the *Sadhak* begins to doubt himself, his goal, and his methods despite sincere endeavours.

In these moments of despair, Faith becomes the sole anchor that holds him steady amidst the storm of uncertainty. He must remind himself that many great Souls have experienced similar temporary stages of despondency and that he will attain the ideal through perseverance. He must endure this suffocating despair, looking beyond it with unwavering hope.

Then, often without warning, the Veil parts—and after his prolonged struggle, the *Sadhak* may suddenly experience a subtle touch of coolness, a moment of Grace that arrives unexpectedly.

This Heavenly touch, though brief, transcends the immediate horizon, infusing the *Sadhak* with light, peace, and strength. In that moment, all doubts and dejection vanish.

Though fleeting, this experience is beyond value or comparison, leaving a lasting impression on *Sadhak's* Consciousness. It recurs at intervals—sometimes short, sometimes long, and with each recurrence, it lingers a little longer, gradually spreading its Light within him.

Even as the *Sadhak* experiences these moments of Grace, the instruments of Mind, Body, and Life continue to function according to their habitual tendencies. Their desires, struggles, victories, and defeats persist, as these are the rhythms of the Lower Nature.

As time passes and the momentum of past actions begins to wane, the power of the instruments of Lower Nature on the *Sadhak* also becomes inactive and dormant, as if they realise that they cannot sustain their activities without the active consent of the *Purusha.* They begin to understand that He, not his Lower Nature, is their true Master. This Realisation initiates a profound transformation within the *Gunas.*

## The Divine Alchemy: Transmuting the *Gunas*

At this advanced stage, the transformation occurs within the instruments themselves.

*Tamas—the quality of inertia and darkness—is transmuted into Divine Poise, a calm and steady equilibrium.*

*Rajas—the quality of passion and restlessness—is transformed into Divine Activity, an energy that is dynamic yet harmoniously aligned with the Higher Will.*

*Sattva—the quality of purity and light—evolves into Divine Illumination, shedding the egoic attachment to virtue and knowledge, and becoming a pure expression of the Divine Light.*

In this Alchemy of Transformation, *Sadhak's* journey is no longer a struggle against the Lower Nature but a harmonious unfolding of the Divine within. Once resistant and rebellious, the instruments now reveal something of the Divine, aligning themselves with the *Purusha's* Will. The *Sadhak* realises that this journey, though fraught with challenges, is guided by an underlying certainty: the inevitable manifestation of the Divine in every aspect of his being.

Thus, the four pillars—Peace, Prayer, Righteousness, and Meditation—serve not merely as practices, but as gateways to the Divine.

# CHAPTER 10

# The Technique of Prayer

Some disciplines are classified as sciences, while others are classified as arts. Yet a few—like Logic and Worship—transcend this divide, drawing upon both the laws of knowledge and the refinements of expression. Their framework belongs to science, but their execution becomes art. Prayer, above all, unites the *certainties* of understanding with the *subtleties* of feeling, weaving science and art into a living synthesis.

Understanding the subtle laws that govern the inner life—both Psychological and Spiritual—brings clarity to the seeker's journey. These laws are not to be obeyed unthinkingly, but studied, tested, and inwardly verified. They offer *direction*, not *dictation.* With them, the path grows less obscure, and the traveller walks with greater poise.

A seeker explores Prayer, not merely as ritual or aspiration, but as a gradual unfolding of the Soul's movement toward the Eternal.

## Role of Worship

Ordinarily, human life is governed by emotions, impulses, and sentiments. While reason may occasionally intervene, it is often shaped—or swayed—by passion, prejudice, and desire. Pure reason alone cannot refine human nature unless that nature itself is prepared to cooperate. This transformation requires an alchemy of the heart—a process awakened through Worship.

The goal of Worship is not meant to intellectualise the Divine but to realise Him. The *sheaths of desires*, egoism, vanity, greed, jealousy, restlessness, fear, and sorrow that surround the heart are shed in Worship, and the heart stands bare before the Divine—unmasked and unguarded.

A *Sadhak* who enters the domain of Worship with a clear heart instantly realises that what he feared to reveal to the Divine is already known. He is seen as a whole, with all his ignorance, egoism, longings, and imperfections. Such Worship, which ultimately leads to a Divine Communion, leaves the seeker enveloped in pure Compassion. The *Sadhak* realises that he is not facing a judging sovereign, but an Eternal Kin. That trust—quiet, direct, and Luminous—is the beginning of Worship.

However, to enter the realm of Worship, the *Sadhak* must first approach God through resonant qualities of love, mercy, grace, and kindness. Just as man is not only his body but bears Divinity, so God is not only the Absolute but also bears Humanity within Himself. The *Upanishad* affirms: *"One must worship God as the dearest beloved."* The sentiment one feels for parents, friends, or mentors must expand, rise, and be redirected—towards the Divine.

In cultivating such sacred intimacy and affectionate nearness to the Divine, there lurks a subtle peril—the peril of drawing God down to the level of the worshipper, rather than the worshipper rising in consciousness towards the Splendour of the Divine. The devotee, instead of striving to purify and correct himself, drifts into the beguiling illusion that the Infinite, in His boundless compassion, condones his grave errors and overlooks even his transgressions and depravities. Emboldened by this mistaken notion of Divine indulgence, he begins to take undue liberty with the Grace that was meant to uplift him. He indulges in fanciful imaginings of God's constant favour, believing that all he does carries the seal of Divine sanction. Gradually, he comes to identify his will and his erring ways with the Supreme Will itself. And when reality shatters this illusion, he turns in bitterness and reproach towards the very Divinity he presumed to possess. Thus, many devout persons have faltered and fallen into this grievous error.

True Prayer does not seek the fulfilment of one's will but the revelation of God's. The goal is to realise His Presence, to dwell in Communion, and allow Him to steer the *Chariot of Life.* This is not a sentimental attachment; it is surrendered awareness.

To worship God as the Mother, though tender and sweet, is not very helpful in the early stages of *Sadhana.* The child too easily exploits the Mother's indulgent nature, shirking discipline and avoiding self-correction. The concept of God as Mother is best reserved for a more mature and illumined stage of *Spiritual Growth.* Initially, it is far more beneficial to envision the Divine as Father, Teacher, Disciplinarian, Taskmaster, and the august and impartial Judge. In this way, the *Sadhak* learns obedience with reverential awe and grows under the purifying flame of *Spiritual Discipline.*

The root of much disappointment in the seeker's journey lies in the failure to awaken the deep conviction that he is the Soul, distinct from the outer instruments—*the triple sheaths of Body, Life, and Mind.* Pouring pure milk into an unclean vessel spoils the milk; likewise, if the *Body, Life, and Mind* are not purified, disciplined, and trained, all higher experiences are tainted by these impure instruments.

While the vulnerable mind adds its own twist and colour to higher truths, the ego may misinterpret an unusual thought as God's voice, or mistake abnormal visions for the Realisation of God.

## Stages of Prayer

Prayer is not merely the act of speaking—it is the *Art of Attunement.* It is the invisible bridge between the Finite and the

Infinite, through which the Soul finds comfort, direction, and Liberation. In times of trial or tribulation, it becomes a transformative force, leading us from the turmoil of life to the Peace of Divine Grace. The forms and intentions of Prayer evolve, reflecting the Spiritual growth of the devotee and his journey towards surrender and Enlightenment. Prayer and aspiration should progress in a step-by-step, stage-by-stage manner.

***Prayer for Relief:*** This Prayer should be simple, seeking relief from a specific situation. In moments of helplessness, one may cry, *"Lift me out of this difficulty."* Such a Prayer is natural when the burden exceeds one's present strength. Yet even here, the appeal must not dictate terms. One should not prescribe how the difficulty should be removed, but trust that God will resolve it in His own way. *"Thou knowest best"* must be its quiet undertone. If Peace follows the Prayer, or there is a sense that a great burden has been lifted, it is the first answer. Sometimes, though, the answer is silence—or delay. Impatience, then, becomes an unnecessary burden.

***Prayer for Strength:*** A higher petition comes with the words, *"Grant me the strength, courage, and wisdom to face this."* Here, the seeker does not ask life to change, but to be changed inwardly. He seeks not escape, but endurance. He calls upon the Divine, as Arjuna did, not to slay the enemy for him, but to stand by his side.

***Prayer for Liberation:*** A still higher Prayer is, *"Liberate me from the cause of all sorrow, misery, and helplessness. Lead me from untruth to Truth, from the Darkness of Ignorance into the Light of Wisdom, from separation from Thee into Life Eternal in Thee. Enable me to distinguish between the shadow and the substance, the Not-Self and the Self, the Impermanent and the Permanent, fleeting fancies and real values of Life, the Perishable and the Imperishable, the Body and the Soul."*

At this stage, the devotee should surrender all gains and losses, pleasures and pains, talents and weaknesses to God, with the firm Faith that all is Divine play, saying, *"Thy Will be done."*

## Understanding Divine Qualities

Many words used in human relationships—goodness, kindness, mercy, protection, love, grace—are also used in our relationship with the Divine. Yet applied to man, these words often imply personal favour or advantage. The moment a person's virtue appears to go against our self-interest, we withdraw the word and call him an enemy

With God, these words must be understood differently. Endeavours toward a Godly life and God-Realisation always carry His blessings, support, and guidance.

Divine Mercy does not mean exemption from pain; Divine Protection does not ensure the absence of trials. A life anchored in God is not necessarily one strewn with roses. Those who walk the *Path of Spirit* face far more ordeals than the worldly. For God's Grace is not always that which saves us from the shipwreck—it may well be that which lets us sink, while all others are spared, so that we may find a greater salvation in the depths. The sincere devotee learns that the path grows steeper not despite *Grace,* but because of it.

## Progressive Stages of Prayer

In a more illumined stage, the aspirant begins to see God's hidden hand in past events. *"As I look back, I discern Thy silent finger moving behind those experiences. Without Thy Will, they could not have touched me. Now grant me the vision to see Thy guidance in the present moment. Let me think, feel, and act in rhythm with Thy Will. Sharpen my inner ear to hear Thy whispered suggestions."*

The aspirant, longing to experience the *Divine Presence* in his life, may cry out, *"Thou art providing me with all I require, even before*

*I ask. But Thou art hiding from my view. I want Thee, not Thy gifts. With Thy Presence, I can joyfully accept whatever else I have or lack. If Thou revealest Thyself to me, even for a moment, I can gladly bear the burden of life and carry out Thy command."*

At this stage, the aspirant should meditate on God's Omnipresence, seeing the *Divine Spirit* in every visible thing. He should perceive God as the Formless within Form, the Impersonal within the Personal, the Changeless within Change, and the Law governing the sequence of events. God is like sight to the eye, light to the lamp, life to the body, thought to the Mind, sound in the ether, sense in sound, fire in wood, music in the flute, and honey in the flower.

A higher stage is realising God's Inner Nature within oneself. The aspirant aspires with the call, *"I find no peace in seeing Thy Glory only in the works of Nature, events of history, lives of great men, or destinies of nations. Grant me the vision to see Thee in my Soul. Remove the 'Maya' that hides Thy Inner Nature."*

Power, Law, and Beauty are outer forms of God's revelation; Peace, Love, Joy, Harmony, Wisdom, Truth, Holiness, and Unity are forms of His Inner Nature.

## The Final Steps

*Aspiration*, *Invitation*, and *Surrender* are the pillars of the effort to realise God. A sincere, burning aspiration is essential—but more is needed. The Aspirant must persistently invite God to dwell within, converting the body into a temple and purifying it—especially the heart—to make it a fit abode for the *Divine.*

*"When the knots of the heart are loosened, the mortal becomes Immortal. This alone is the teaching." — Mundaka Upanishad, 2.2.8*

Invitation gains meaning through Surrender. Surrender must be total, integral, and unconditional—without any part of the devotee resisting it. Thought, feeling, sentiment, emotion, will, instinct, and ego must learn to obey the *Divine* without reservation. God gives Himself to those who wholly surrender themselves to Him. Surrender is not merely a physical gesture, like prostration, but a subduing of the lower instincts of Body, Life, Mind, and Ego to the impulses of the *Divine.*

## True Offering

Man often attempts to please God with material offerings. Yet God does not desire our possessions, words, works, or even our ideals. What God seeks is the Inner Being—attuned to the rhythm of *Nature,* participating in Cosmic Life, sharing in others' sorrows, offering others a share of our joys, elevating Consciousness, and demonstrating the capacity for sacrifice. The purpose of good works and noble ideals is only to expand and uplift Consciousness.

In the early stages of spiritual growth, one's concept of God is often limited to a possessive and personal relationship. God is *'my God'.* Just as a child is possessive of his mother and cannot bear others calling her 'mother,' so too the devotee initially clings to this exclusive bond with the Divine.

However, as *Spiritual Understanding* deepens, a quiet transformation takes place. The devotee begins to rejoice when others share in this relationship, just as the child eventually delights in the *Universal Motherhood* of the mother. The personal God becomes the God of all.

In these advanced stages, the devotee perceives the Divine Presence even in others' gods, recognising aspects of his own ideals reflected in their beliefs and practices. This broadened perspective fosters a deep sense of unity, where one sees oneself in others and others in oneself.

The devotee comes to realise that the *Divine Mother* manifests Herself to Her children in many forms and through different paths. Just as a mother relates to the same child in various ways at different stages of life, so too does the *Divine* reveal Herself differently to each seeker, according to their level of understanding and need.

The aspirant must cultivate this expansive and inclusive attitude from the beginning. Without it, there is a risk of falling into bigotry, fanaticism, and a narrow, one-sided view of spirituality. Such limitations can lead to an exaggerated and disproportionate development of devotion, where one perceives disharmony in the Divine attributes.

True Spiritual growth reveals the harmony of God's Will in the workings of Nature, the alignment between the devotee's intentions and the Divine plan, and the Universe as an expression of Divine Will. The devotee experiences *Inner Ecstasy* and the workings of a higher force moving through and within himself. These are the fruits of sincere aspiration— Prayer and Devotion. Thus, Prayer ceases to be a plea and becomes Presence—not our voice reaching upward, but the Eternal Whispering within.

# CHAPTER 11

# *Sadhana:* The Sage's Vigil

या निशा सर्वभूतानां तस्यां जागर्ति संयमी।
यस्यां जाग्रति भूतानि सा निशा पश्यतो मुनेः॥

*When people of the world are fast asleep, the sage is wide awake. When the worldly-minded are awake, the sage is in deep sleep. — Bhagavad Gita 2.69.*

This verse marks the inward divergence between two ways of living. Where the world moves from unrest, seeking fulfilment in the fleeting, the awakened one lives from stillness, anchored in what endures. What the world celebrates as gain, the seer often recognises as bondage. This is not a condemnation. It is a quiet witnessing of lives oriented by differing truths.

The *Sadhak*, while not yet established in that stillness, walks the path with growing discernment. He begins to turn away from the glare of surface living and seeks that which does not perish with time. Slowly, his lens shifts—from attraction to awareness, from reaction to reflection. That which is clung to by the multitude begins to lose its charm, and the Soul turns inward, drawn to something subtler, vaster, and truer.

## The Role of the Ideal in Life

The Ideal is a guiding light, greater and higher than Life itself. Life, in turn, becomes a means, an occasion, and an opportunity to realise this Ideal. The Ideal is not the highest Truth, surpassing the Mind, but rather a mental concept—a distant flash of Truth, an intimation from beyond, a twilight of understanding. A Life without an Ideal is a purposeless struggle, a journey without a destination, a movement without direction, and an experience without significance. Once this Ideal is glimpsed, Life begins to organise around it.

The first distinction made by one who has an Ideal is between what is Eternal and what is transient. This leads to further divisions—what is important and unimportant, what is more or less significant, and what constitutes normal versus special duty, *'saamaanya dharma'* versus *'visesha dharma'*. Every aspect of Life is viewed through the lens of how it serves or reveals the Ideal. The idealist loves the Idea in things and serves the *Spirit in the Idea*. An Ideal gives Life direction, meaning, and significance, setting the idealist's outlook apart from those without such guidance. *'Lakshya Suddhi, Chitta Suddhi, Sadhana Suddhi'*—purity of the Ideal, the Mind, and the means are necessary for the attainment of Divinity. Life becomes a tension between what is and what ought to be.

Godhood represents the Ultimate Ideal, encompassing and surpassing all other ideals. It embraces all Human instincts and fields of Life. Yet, as aspirants strive to live according to the Ideal, they face a barrage of influences and subtleties that must be corrected, purified, sublimated, or firmly rejected.

## Materialism and Dogmatism

These resistances faced by the *Sadhak* are not forces waging war upon him; they are familiar patterns—ways of seeing, desiring, and evaluating—that no longer serve the unfolding of higher awareness. Two subtle outlooks often surface early: Materialism and Dogmatism.

Materialism is not simply an attachment to possessions; it is a narrowing of Reality to the measurable. It insists that only what is perceptible through the senses or useful for enjoyment is real or worthwhile. From this perspective, life is an economy of pleasures and utilities. Loftier concepts such as Truth, Sacrifice, or Inner Growth seem impractical or naïve to a materialist. Even virtues are weighed only for their transactional value.

Dogmatism, though opposite in appearance, works in a parallel way. It affirms belief in the Divine but seeks to replace Inner Transformation with *external assurance,* such as ritual, affiliation, or unquestioning dedication to a doctrine or teacher. It reduces Spiritual Life to repetition, mistaking obedience for Salvation, and intellectual submission for true Inner Surrender.

In both tendencies, the living Presence of the Divine is bypassed—one by denial, the other by distortion. The *Sadhak* must recognise them for what they are: provisional stages of Consciousness. Neither arises from malice; both reflect his unripe longing for security, certainty, and comfort. To outgrow them, the *Sadhak* needs neither argument nor rebellion, but a quiet fidelity to Truth. By holding fast to the Ideal and by examining these tendencies without fear or attachment, he slowly releases their hold. He reawakens the deeper aspiration that first set him on the Path.

## The Inner Ordeal and the Graceful Ascent

Even as the *Sadhak* makes sincere progress, challenges do not vanish—they shift. Old tendencies may fall away, but subtler imbalances emerge. Success in restraint may give rise to Spiritual pride; humility may turn into passivity, and Devotion into attachment. What served him in earlier stages may begin to veil the Truth at higher ones. This is not regression, but refinement—the purification of even his virtues, until only what is essential remains.

The Path is not linear. A moment of vigilance may be followed by fatigue, a burst of clarity by confusion. There are days of effort and days of stillness—times when aspiration glows bright, and times when it dims into silence. These variations are not signs of failure but of deepening Transformation. The *Sadhak* learns not to judge the journey by surface rhythms, but by the quiet unfolding of Inner Poise.

He begins to perceive that behind his striving, another Presence is at work. What once felt like a solitary ascent slowly becomes a quiet collaboration between human will and Divine Movement. The Divine does not impose Himself; He waits until the will of the *Sadhak* grows still, ready to be guided, and his motives are clear enough to be trusted. In that surrender, the *Sadhak* does not lose the capacity to choose and act, but he gains a deeper alignment with the Truth of his being.

This surrender is not passive; it is an alert offering. The *Sadhak's* quest does not end—his vigilance remains, his sincerity deepens. But now he walks with the quiet assurance that the strength he needs does not come solely from himself. There is guidance—not always visible, not always comforting, but always present.

To walk this path is to accept the slow rhythms of real change, to embrace the solitude without self-pity, and to offer one's Will without self-assertion. The *Sadhak* does not arrive at some distant end—he is gradually, inwardly claimed by the Divine whom he sought. And in that silent claiming, he recognises not only the goal, but the One who walked beside him all along.

# CHAPTER 12

# Freedom of Spirit

What bestows dignity and decency upon the human personality? It is not the size and beauty of the body, nor learning and intelligence, nor artistic talent or skill in execution, nor even holding a prominent position. These are qualities that even those of ignoble character may possess. It is goodness, an expression of Godliness, that grants dignity to man.

Throughout history, the educated, intelligent, and artistically talented people in the world have consistently outnumbered those with goodness. Here, 'good' refers to a powerful and transformative goodness, distinct from the goodness born out of helplessness or despair. Similarly, efforts to awaken and evolve the goodness in man have been greater than those aimed at merely educating him. Various concepts, such as heaven and hell, the law of *Karma*, rewards, and punishments in this life and the next, and codes of conduct, have been upheld with high hopes. Yet man's progress in goodness remains slow.

The Earth would not bear such sufferings if truly good people were abundant. All knowledge, ability, and artistic genius have often served the Devil within.

## *Tamas, Rajas*—and Ego

To be powerful and effective, goodness must be free from the domination of *Tamas*—inertia, ignorance, and *Rajas*—egoism, restlessness. Understanding the manifestations of these forces in life and mind is crucial for liberation.

In the evolutionary unfolding of Creation, matter appeared first, forming the substratum of existence. Life then emerged as movement within matter, and Mind arose later as a subtler articulation of consciousness. However, the Mind does not function independently; it remains conditioned by the impulses of matter and life, which often assert precedence in shaping its direction. Until these layers are integrated within awareness, their friction may manifest as inner conflict—when physical comfort clashes with conscience, or when biological instinct overpowers contemplative Mind. Such disharmonies are not signs of failure, but invitations to harmonise these domains in the light of the Self. Integration is not achieved by denial, but by quiet Illumination—an inner vision that gently reveals the unity beneath apparent conflict.

In the earliest stages of human evolution, the physical body and its needs held paramount importance. Strength, stature, and visible prowess commanded respect. Those who could consume the most, display the greatest endurance, and those who could confront wild beasts became revered icons. What stirred *instinct* was valued above what stirred *reflection.* What appeared to the eye was held to be more real than what was perceived through sound, and what could be grasped with the hand was believed to be reality itself. Beauty, too, was confined to bodily form—what lay beyond direct sensory experience was dismissed as intangible and thus insignificant. Abstract thought had no place in a world governed by immediacy and survival.

Although that age ended long ago, its impressions linger in the unconscious of the human race. The fanciful imaginations, fantastic beliefs, superstitions, hopes, and fears often reflected even among those in positions of influence reveal traces of the Stone Age. Attachment to one's birthplace, blind adherence to tradition, mechanical observance of rituals, unjustifiable reverence for the old, apprehensions about the future, reluctance to change, herd mentality, laziness, and yielding to bodily instincts are signs of the lingering influence of *Tamas,* the principle of inertia.

## The Influence of *Rajas*

*Rajas*, one of the three *Gunas* of Nature, is intimately tied to the vital aspect of man. It expresses itself through restlessness, ambition, possessiveness, jealousy, intolerance, and even cruelty. Under its influence, a person may struggle with sleeplessness and emotional agitation, feeling disturbed by another's good fortune and oddly gratified by a rival's misfortune. The thought of wealth, status, or social dominance brings intense excitement; conversely, the loss of these symbols of power plunges one into sorrow and collapse.

While the idea of possession nourishes the vital being—the aspect of human nature driven by emotion and desire—the physical being seeks gratification through the actual experience and physical indulgence.

For the vital being, life itself is the end, saturated with emotional highs and lows, attachments and aversions. However, for the Mind, life is a means: a pathway for reflection, *discrimination*, and *ascent*.

This divergence between the vital nature and the *Manomaya Purusha* gives rise to an inward tension, not a battle, but a subtle conflict of orientation. The vital nature does not readily yield; it seeks dominance, craves movement, and resists inner stillness. Yet the *Manomaya Purusha*—the Mental Self, the indwelling person in the mind—is not its adversary. He stands apart, not in rejection, but in quiet readiness to guide. As the *Sadhak* takes sincere steps on the Path, he begins to recognise that these two aspects need not oppose each other. Through patient engagement—much like educating a talented yet untamed student—the Mind must reveal to the vital being the dignity and joy of a higher life. When understanding replaces coercion, Inner Harmony emerges. The elements begin to move as one, no longer fragmented, but unified in their journey toward the Self.

## The Role of the Ego

The Mind, too, has its limitations. As *Tamas* and *Rajas* are brought under its control, a strong individuality becomes necessary, often assuming the form of the ego. Unlike the Soul, which is a uniting entity, the ego is a dividing and separating principle. The ego serves as Nature's instrument for diversification and differentiation. In this process, man often mistakes the ego for the *Soul*—a spark of the Divine and the self-expressing centre-point of God. He fears that losing his ego would render him a cypher. Consequently, he clings to his newfound power. He tries to strengthen, protect, and fortify it. He is prepared to make any sacrifice and face any ordeal in this direction.

## Aspiring for the Divine

The aspirant or the *Sadhak* encounters many subtle pitfalls along the Path within his own evolving awareness. To navigate them, he must first learn to distinguish the Soul's quiet guidance from the ego's restless claims. When he finds himself elated by praise or shaken by failure, it is often the ego that has stepped forward, which he may mistake for the *Soul*. These fluctuations he experiences are not deviations, but phases in the rhythm of inner growth. What matters is not the absence of change, but the presence of equanimity.

Equanimity does not mean indifference to good and evil, nor does it imply moral neutrality. It is a *poised awareness* that remains steady amid gain and loss, pleasure and pain, while still upholding the good and resisting the false. The ego, subtle and persistent, may assume many forms—sometimes crude, sometimes refined. It may even echo the voice of the Divine, not to uplift, but to mislead. The aspirant must remain vigilant, not with suspicion, but with sincerity.

Reason, too, is a noble faculty—capable of discerning Truth from illusion within the limits of the Mind. But when it reaches the threshold of higher consciousness, it falters. It cannot grasp the Transformative force that lies beyond its range. At that point, it must not be discarded, but *refined*—made receptive through humility, attunement, and quiet expectancy. Then, it becomes a channel for Illumination rather than a barrier to it.

As the quest of the *Sadhak* deepens, the Mind itself begins to aspire—not merely to understand, but to behold. It seeks to perceive the Divine not as a concept, but as a Presence: in the rhythm of events, in the beauty of form, in the compassion that underlies all movement. The Universe begins to appear not as a collection of objects, but as a field of *Rasa*—of essence—suffused with Compassion, and Light, where each moment reveals the touch of the Divine.

Through sustained aspiration, the Mind is gradually transformed. It no longer stands apart, analysing; it begins to participate. And as it opens, the physical and vital parts of the *Sadhak* are also drawn upward. They become instruments—not of desire, but of revelation. The Divine does not descend with thunder; He enters through readiness. And when the whole being is aligned, even the simplest act becomes a gesture of the *Eternal.*

When the *Inner Being* is aligned and the Divine begins to move through thought, feeling, and act, the *Sadhak* no longer walks alone. Yet the journey does not end in stillness—it must extend into life. For what the *Soul* realises in silence must find expression in the world. This is where the teachings of the *Bhagavad Gita* become luminous, revealing how such action becomes Sacred—not by withdrawal, but by participation without claim; not by renunciation of the world, but by immersion without bondage.

*Having glimpsed the Eternal, the Sadhak learns to move as its instrument.*

# CHAPTER 13

# Divine Dynamics in the Gita

The *Bhagavad Gita*, often called the *Song Celestial*, is not merely a scripture—it is a living dialogue between the Eternal and the evolving *Soul*. It stands as a Luminous embodiment of *Vedanta* applied to the realities of daily life. Long before its revelation, profound Spiritual *Truths* had been proclaimed, yet they remained largely confined to the realm of *Inner Realisation*.

*Vedanta* was long regarded as a philosophy of transcendence, rather than one of engagement. Its emphasis on renunciation led many to believe that Spiritual Life required withdrawal from the world.

This created a quiet divide: the inner and the outer, the contemplative and the active, the sage and the householder. The methods of Realisation appeared diverse, even conflicting, and the seeker was left wondering whether life was a distraction or a field for growth.

The *Gita* resolved this tension. It declared that *Vedanta* is not a retreat from life, but a way of living it with depth, clarity, and surrender. It harmonised the paths of knowledge, devotion, and action into a *unified vision* of Spiritual Evolution.

## From Renunciation to Dynamic Living

Traditionally, *Quietism*—a serene detachment from the world—was regarded as the highest Spiritual state. The universe was seen as a passing shadow, and life as a transient illusion. While this attitude preserved inner peace, it often led to the neglect of values, responsibilities, and the richness of human experience. In some cases, it contributed to cultural stagnation and the decline of civilisations.

The *Gita's* message arose as a corrective to this imbalance. It affirmed that passivity and inaction are not the hallmarks of the highest Truth. Rather, they represent an incomplete understanding of existence.

The *Gita's* uniqueness lies in its choice of setting—a battlefield. In selecting the chaos of war as the backdrop for its teachings, it makes a bold statement: if *Vedanta* can illuminate the heart in the midst of battle, it can illuminate human beings in every aspect of life. The battlefield becomes a metaphor for the human condition, where choices must be made, duties fulfilled, and values upheld—despite uncertainty and pain.

The battlefield, where man confronts his most primal instincts, becomes the crucible for the *Bhagavad Gita's* transformative message. In this crucible, he is stripped of sentiment and forced to act without personal malice or vendetta. It teaches that both rest and work, as well as wisdom and dynamism, are essential for a balanced life. Without its teachings, the *Upanishads* would remain incomplete, lofty in vision but lacking in application. The *Gita* integrates their insights into a living philosophy of action, where the Divine is not only realised in silence but expressed through movement.

## Spiritual Nourishment

It is beautifully said: *The Upanishads are cows, Krishna is the cowherd, and the Gita is the milk*. Arjuna was the first to drink this nourishing essence, and countless seekers have followed, finding strength, clarity, and solace in its teachings. Arjuna's despair on the battlefield mirrors the existential crises faced by many—a moment when the intellect fails, the will falters, and the heart is overwhelmed.

In such moments, the *Gita* becomes a beacon. It does not offer escape, but Illumination. It begins with the most fundamental inquiry: *Who am I? What am I not?* These questions are not philosophical abstractions—they are the keys to freedom. When the seeker gains clarity, illusions dissolve like mist before the rising sun. He realises that the body, life, and mind are instruments—not the Self. The true Self is Divine, Eternal, and infinitely potent.

Establishing oneself in this awareness is not a retreat from life—it is the foundation for engaging with it wisely and boldly. Self-knowledge brings energy, joy, and confidence. It enables one to stand above his problems—not by ignoring them, but by seeing them in the light of his deeper nature.

## *Karma Yoga*: The Path of Divine Action

However, merely establishing oneself in the Consciousness of the Divine nature is not enough. The *Gita* insists that one must act—work must continue until the last breath. Inaction is not liberation; it is stagnation, yet *Gita's* profound teaching of action in inaction reveals that true renunciation lies not in withdrawal, but in the spirit with which one engages. *Gita* views life and worldly matters from a Divine perspective.

*Karma Yoga* bridges the Secular and the Sacred. It transforms every act into a Spiritual offering. It begins with Truth and moves toward greater truths. In *Karma Yoga*, serving God and seeing God are simultaneous. The Divine becomes not a distant abstraction, but a Living Presence in work.

*Karma Yoga* does not demand prior attainment or specialised knowledge—it begins wherever the seeker stands. Its strength lies in its capacity to integrate the Spiritual with the everyday, allowing the body to act, the emotions to mature, and the Mind to clarify through conscious engagement. In this path, work is not merely a duty but a means of inner refinement. Through sustained action offered without attachment, the *Sadhak* gradually aligns his outer life with his inner aspiration.

The rhythm of *Karma Yoga* brings a quiet order—not enforced, but awakened—within the individual and, by extension, within the collective. Devotion, discernment, and selflessness are not imposed ideals here; they emerge naturally as the Soul begins to act in harmony with its deeper Truth.

To the *Karmayogin*, the universe is not a material construct. Matter is merely the outermost layer. Beneath it lies a *field of Consciousness*, waiting to be awakened through purposeful action.

## *Swadharma*: The Law of One's Being

Another invaluable teaching of the *Gita* is the concept of *Swadharma*, the law of one's being. Each individual is born with a unique constitution, a distinct mould shaped by past evolution and present potential. To discover this mould through introspection and to act in harmony with it is the essence of Spiritual Living and the manifestation of the Divine within.

*Swadharma* is not confined to one's profession, caste, or social role. It transcends external labels and reaches into the *Soul's blueprint*. It is a personal mandate—an inner calling that aligns with the greater good. By reflecting on one's tendencies, strengths, and stage of growth, one can discern the Path that leads to fulfilment and transformation.

Mechanical adherence to tradition cannot replace this inner discernment. True progress arises from conscious alignment—not blind conformity. *Swadharma* invites the seeker to live authentically, to honour his nature, and to evolve through it—not despite it. It is not a rigid law, but a living rhythm—one that changes as the Soul deepens. To follow *Swadharma* is to walk in step with one's own Truth, and thereby with the Divine.

## Surrender and Liberation

Perhaps the most Luminous note in the *Gita* is its assurance of Liberation through Surrender. This Surrender is not a gesture of weakness—it is the culmination of wisdom. It must be total, encompassing all desires, fears, gains, losses, and identities. The ego, which masquerades as the Self, must be gently laid aside. It served its purpose, but now the time has come to replace *I* and *Mine* with the Consciousness of *Thou* and *Thine*.

When surrender is complete, the seeker enters a state of quiet trust, not dependence in the worldly sense, but confident attunement. It is an inner repose born of fidelity to the *Divine*. The burden of control is released into a *Wisdom* that sees beyond the mind and deeper than the will. A mind free from anxiety is not indifferent—it is in Spiritual repose.

Such surrender must be offered to the One alone, without division of loyalty, without ambiguity of allegiance. When the will of the seeker aligns wholly with the rhythm of the Supreme, it is not submission—it is concord. This inner harmony, where no resistance remains between the *Soul's* movement and the *Divine unfolding*, is the quiet splendour of *jivanmukti*: liberation in the midst of life.

The central theme of the *Bhagavad Gita* is the recognition that each individual must rely on himself for upliftment and work out his destiny. External help may be beneficial, but it cannot substitute for direct experience. The forces that uplift or degrade lie within, for man is both his own best friend and his own worst enemy. Liberation is thus not a gift—it is a personal attainment.

*Gita* teaches that man can counteract planetary influences, neutralise *karmic* pressures, and remain untouched by societal or political turbulence. The Divine resides within, making each individual the architect of his destiny. This self-reliance is the foundation of Spiritual growth, and believing that external forces cause misery is a sign of mental immaturity. Through self-knowledge, self-effort, and surrender, the seeker becomes not only free but Luminous.

*Gita's message is one of empowerment. It does not promise ease—it offers strength. It does not remove struggle—it reveals its purpose.*

# CHAPTER 14

# Pilgrimage

Sometimes, we see birds perched on telegraph wires—chirping, perhaps in quiet communication. They rest for a few moments before swiftly taking flight. To them, these wires are nothing more than a temporary perch. They remain unaware of the powerful energy coursing through those cables.

Likewise, we often dwell upon the surface of *consciousness,* skimming the uppermost layers of the mind. We remain oblivious to the profound depths of our being—the latent powers of the Mind, the constant influences of environmental consciousness, and the higher plans decreed beyond our mental plane. The capacities of surface awareness may suffice for worldly endeavours, yet they fall short in revealing the ultimate Truth of Existence or in providing enduring peace.

## The Surface and the Depths

The Mind is a marvellous mechanism. What is it? We do not see it, yet we do not doubt its reality. Is the Mind solid, liquid, or a gas? In one moment, it laughs and feels proud; in another, it weeps and feels dejected.

If the external universe astonishes us, the Mind dazzles even more. If there is mystery in the universe, the Mind harbours deeper enigmas. If great powers operate in the cosmos, even greater powers stir within the Mind. In its vastness lie baffling contradictions—more confounding than those of the galaxies.

## The Duality Within

Our thoughts, dreams, inhibitions, complexes, angularities, suppressed instincts, and sudden outbursts offer but a glimpse of the commotion the *Mind* can create. The most devastating tragedies, catastrophic events, and fiercest wars first ignite in the Minds of men. Yet it is also here that the loftiest visions are born—acts of compassion, flashes of genius, revelations that uplift entire civilisations. The Mind is a crucible where both the Divine and the Demon dwell, its possibilities nearly limitless. Milton's insight remains timeless: *"The Mind can make a Heaven of Hell and a Hell of Heaven."*

The *Bhagavad Gita* echoes this Eternal Truth:

*"Thou art thy best well-wisher, and thou art thy worst enemy. So, uplift thyself with the help of thyself."*

## The Microcosm—Macrocosm

All that the universe holds resides within man. As a single drop of water reflects the entirety of the Ganges, so too does man mirror the universe. The outer world is the macrocosm; the Mind, its microcosmic counterpart. His body is composed of the same constituents that pervade the cosmos—mineral, vegetal, animal, and spiritual—each layer echoing a dimension of existence. His breath pulses in rhythm with the boundless flow of life, and his Mind, though seemingly individual, is in truth a fragment of the Universal Intelligence—a spark kindled from the vast fire of Consciousness. Every aspect of his being draws nourishment from the Grand Whole.

Science views the Mind as the functional power of the brain. Spiritual insight, however, sees the brain as the Mind's chosen vessel—a medium through which it expresses its knowing. These perspectives, though divergent in approach, contemplate the same truth from opposite ends.

Mind arises later in the evolutionary sequence. Yet this temporal emergence affirms its primacy in essence, for it remains nearer to the fountainhead of Being. It transcends the universe that gave rise to it—knowing its laws, uncovering its secrets, and harnessing its forces. The Mind is the knower; the universe, the known. Through its capacity to reflect, discern, and intuit, the Mind stands closer to the source of Existence. It is through the Mind that God works most directly, revealing that behind matter stands Consciousness—subtle, Luminous, and Supreme.

## The Illusion of the External

We stand in awe of the outer world—our own creation—forgetting the quiet grandeur of the Self. An ant, moved by its own will, surpasses a rail engine that depends on borrowed force. Enchanted by form, power, and visibility, we feel diminished, as though eclipsed by our own shadow. This tendency to exalt the gross and dismiss the subtle is devastating when it extends inward, and more attention is given to the body than to the Mind, to the seen than to the unseen.

*It is the invisible that governs all visibility. Subtlety is strength; the finer the essence, the more potent its power.*

The ideal of every noble culture is to awaken man to his true strength—to inspire him to recognise that he is greater than his desires, stronger than his problems, and sovereign over circumstance.

If there are ghosts, he can dispel them. If *Karma* binds, he can reshape it. If planetary influence is significant, he may be able to transcend it. If society oppresses, he may transform it. If governance proves unsuitable, he may collaborate with others to abolish it. He may work upon himself, upon the world, or both.

Whether inwardly or outwardly, man can be the architect of his destiny.

## Truth in Perspective

This truth finds further support in the nature of *perception* itself. Man's experience of the *universe*—his joys and sorrows—is shaped not solely by what is, but by how the Mind perceives. The world appears as much through the lens of perception as through the reality it conceals.

The Earth seems flat and still beneath his feet—yet this is an illusion born of nearness. From afar, it reveals itself as a sphere in perpetual motion, spinning through space. The stars, serene and watchful in the night sky, awaken in the *Soul* a sense of Divine presence. But they, too, are in motion—racing through the cosmos. Their stillness is not real, but a product of distance.

The observer and the observed cannot be separated. Perception is never passive; it does not merely reflect reality—it actively participates in shaping it. Man's challenge, then, is not only to see clearly, but to see through—to pierce the veil of appearance and awaken to the silent power that moves behind all forms.

A flower may be studied from many perspectives—scientific, artistic, devotional, pragmatic, commercial, or romantic. Our understanding of it depends on the standpoint from which we perceive. To the human eye, things appear one way; to the elephant's eye, another; to the ant's eye, yet another. Which of these perspectives is true? Which is false? All are relatively true—none absolutely.

Scientists speak of the *universe* as governed by stern, impartial, and inexorable laws. Yet *an observed law* does not disclose the secrets of the universe—it only states what cannot be otherwise. It explains the *how* of a thing, but not the *why*.

The concept of law in nature is not an external edict, but a framework discovered by man—a reflection of pattern and order. The recurrence of sunrise and sunset, the rhythm of seasons, the arc of stars—these impressed the observing Mind and were named *"laws"*. Yet no outer power enforces them; the Mind discovers, discerns, and names that which is.

Law is not a tyrant but a mirror. It does not dictate—it reveals. It does not command—it organises. The order we perceive in nature is the order we have found within ourselves.

## Pilgrimage Within

Our inward journey is a *Pilgrimage*—a gradual unfolding of *Consciousness* from the surface to the depths. Along this path, the superficial gives way to the Profound, the fragmented to the Whole, the transient to the *Eternal.*

True Pilgrimage is not about covering physical distances, but bridging the gap between the lower and higher selves. The *Mind,* when tamed and attuned, becomes the sacred vehicle that carries us toward ultimate *Realisation.*

*Thus, the Pilgrimage within is the greatest journey one can undertake—leading to the insight that the Self and the Universe are not two, but one indivisible Whole.*

# CHAPTER 15

# Threefold Realisation

The seeker's journey, though strewn with varied practices and distinct perspectives, is ultimately a pilgrimage toward the One. Whether the path is walked through the illumined clarity of wisdom or the soft devotion of love, the goal remains the same—the Divine, who is both the source and the summit of all Spiritual striving. The ways may differ, the temperaments may vary, but beneath all these diverse movements lies a single yearning: to know, to love, and to become one with That which is Eternal.

The aspirant of knowledge treads the austere path of discernment, peeling away the veils of illusion, layer by layer, in pursuit of the unchanging Truth. This is a path of silent inquiry, of looking beyond the name and the form, the flicker of desire and the storm of thought, until all that remains is the still flame of awareness. The seeker thus learns to distinguish the Real from the unreal, and through repeated contemplation, disidentifies from the body, the life-force, and the restless Mind. These are seen not as the Self, but as instruments of the self—passing masks worn by something deeper. What begins to shine through is the Self-Luminous Essence—Eternal, Self-Existent, untouched by the whirl of Nature.

On the other hand, the devotee moves not by analysis but by surrender. Instead of pulling the veils aside, he places himself entirely in the hands of the Beloved, trusting in His Grace, yearning only for His nearness. With every beat of the heart, he murmurs: *"I am Thine, O Lord. Do with me as Thou wilt."*

In this act of self-offering, the ego melts away like mist before the morning sun. What remains is a *Soul* illumined by love, open as a flower. Whether one says *Soham—"I am That"—or Daasoham—"I am Thy servant"*—the essence realised at the end of either path is the same. Both arrive at the Divine within, one through the precision of Light, the other through the warmth of Fire.

## The Subtle Vision of *Kshara Brahmayoga*

There is a way of seeing in which the world, so often perceived as inert and meaningless, is transformed into a living mystery. In *Kshara Brahmayoga*, the seeker learns to look beyond the surface of things—to glimpse an intelligence shaping events, a beauty radiating from forms, and a hidden purpose behind the play of circumstances. One begins to sense a Divine orchestration not only in moments of grandeur but even in the ordinary rhythms of life.

To achieve this vision, one must gradually transcend the utilitarian view of the world. It is not enough to see objects merely in terms of use, laws, and forces. One must awaken a sensibility that can feel the subtle, an inner receptivity that responds to harmony, to suggestion, to that which is felt but not seen. Emotion becomes a path; aesthetic delight a form of knowing. The *Real* is no longer defined rigidly by what is measurable; it becomes suffused with meaning.

In this deepened gaze, the Universe grows personal. It is no longer a machine, but a Presence. Matter becomes luminous, no longer dead but *ensouled.* The visible and audible world becomes the outermost crust of something Radiant and Conscious. Even events no longer appear accidental. What seems like chance is seen as a thread in a Divine weaving. The very laws of Nature cease to be mechanical—they are recognised as expressions of a Conscious Will, repeating not out of blind necessity, but out of a hidden rhythm of intention.

Such a seeker begins to see life as evolution—not merely of form or complexity, but of Spirit. Pain and pleasure alike become teachers; beauty and terror, twin faces of the same mystery. The world becomes a *mansion of mirrors*, each reflection pointing back to the One Light that plays behind all forms. To the awakened *Soul*, even sorrow has a sacred scent, even silence speaks.

*Every being, however limited or crude, is a carrier of a Secret Flame. Experience becomes the furnace through which the Spirit shapes itself, perfecting and purifying its instruments.*

## The Tender Descent of the Divine

Love always descends to meet the beloved. The mother bends to raise the child and grows in the process. The teacher meets the student's level to guide him, evolving through the act of teaching. The rescuer dives into peril to save another and emerges transformed. So too, the Divine descends—not out of need but Compassion.

Leaving the serene realm of perfection, God descends to walk among the imperfect. In this descending movement, the Divine assumes our limitations. He enters our ignorance not as a judge, but as a redeemer, and *uplifted* by the very act of *uplifting* us. And yet, even as God descends, man ascends. For the heart, touched by Divine nearness, begins to aspire. Aspiration leaps upward like a flame, to meet the downward touch of Grace. This is the *Pathithapavana*—the one who sanctifies the fallen, not by rejection but by embrace. This rhythm—God's descent into man, and man's ascent toward God—is the Eternal dance of Spiritual Life.

The perception of rhythm awakens a new depth of humanity in the seeker—a Compassion no longer born of sympathy, but of identification with the Divine Will. This is *Kshara Purushayoga*—the Realisation of the Divine active in the mutable, the evolving, the many-formed. But this is not yet the whole Truth. *For, to see the Divine in forms is beautiful; to know Him beyond form is liberation.*

## The Deathless and the Desireless

Immortality is not the prolongation of the present form of life. It is the crossing over of the boundary that binds being to cause and effect. It is the passage beyond the Law of death and rebirth, into the realm of pure Spirit. To attain this freedom, one must conquer not only the fear of death but also the clinging to life.

This does not mean a hatred of the world, but a love that is no longer bound by possessions. It is to love as the Divine loves—without clinging, without demanding, without seeking return. It is to stand inwardly free, even in the act of embracing. True liberation belongs to those who have loosened every knot of desire, dissolved the illusions of self-importance, and released themselves from the compulsions of attachment.

The *Upanishad* echoes across the centuries:

*"When all the knots of the heart are severed, the mortal becomes Immortal."*

Such detachment is not dryness but depth. It brings not indifference, but an unshakeable poise. The seeker who meditates regularly upon the indwelling Spirit begins to identify not with the fleeting self but with the Eternal. From that height, even the personality is seen as a passing mask—a movement in time observed from beyond time.

A great stillness then enters. It is like a long, dreamless sleep, yet you are awake. The mind no longer chatters; the will no longer grasps. Peace is no longer a passing state—it becomes the very substance of being.

## *Kshara, Akshara,* and the Hidden Harmony

Some see the Divine only in the play of life—in movement, variety, emotion, and becoming. These walk the path of *Kshara,* where the mutable Divine reveals Himself through forms, contrasts, and relationships. Others transcend movement altogether, entering the stillness beyond all name and quality. These walk the path of *Akshara*, where individuality dissolves into Unity, and even the idea of God may vanish into *Pure Being*.

But the one who sees wholly sees both. The Supreme is not limited to either becoming or being. *He is both, and beyond both.* This is *Purushottama*—the Supreme Person who unites the active and the silent, the manifest and the unmanifest. In the cosmic play, the mutable Soul is the actor, the immutable is the witness, and the Supreme is the Orchestrator—the *Sutradhari* who holds the invisible strings.

## The Flowering of Unity

When the seeker enters *Purushottamayoga*, opposites are no longer at war—they embrace. In the earlier stages, relationships are directed toward God—He is seen as father, mother, guide, friend, and the goal. In the later stages, emotions are transcended. But in the highest stage, all is lived in Communion with Him. Desire is no longer denied nor indulged—it is fulfilled in union. From such a state, action flows naturally—not driven by ambition, nor halted by detachment. One no longer *chooses* to serve; service flows like fragrance from a flower, or light from a flame. Compassion becomes spontaneous, love effortless. One no longer touches to heal; healing happens through Presence. The body becomes a channel; the voice, a vibration of something deeper. Words rise from silence, deeds from stillness—but neither belongs to the doer. The self has vanished into That.

The world is no longer something to escape, nor something to conquer. It is the unfolding of the Divine in time. A Realised Soul does not separate the Spiritual from worldly. To him, the line between Spiritual and worldly dissolves—each moment becomes an act of Worship. Every moment is sacred; every encounter, a meeting with the Divine in one of His myriad forms. The Enlightened person gives without thinking of giving, loves without needing to possess, acts like a wave rising from the sea, with no separate origin. His life speaks what words cannot teach. He is the quiet echo of Grace.

## The Final Realisation

This is not the end of the path, but it is blossoming into life. Philosophy has been transformed into Presence. The seeker who once yearned, now *is*. The world, once seen as a field of bondage or striving, is now the garden of the Spirit, where the Divine is perceived in countless forms.

This is the final flowering—not an escape from the world, but the world itself seen anew. Not a rejection of life, but its sacred consummation. Here, Realisation walks not into retreat, but into rhythm—through the lanes of life, unseen yet Radiant. To this rhythm, the rhythm of the Divine dancing through every breath, we now attune ourselves.

*We do not reach the end. We enter the Beginning.*

# CHAPTER 16

# Stages of Realisation

In a world increasingly engulfed by violence, cruelty, and the erosion of law and moral order, the foundations of human dignity tremble. Hijackings, robberies, and the tragic devastations of domestic abuse and murder have become distressingly commonplace, casting long shadows over the sanctity of life. Each day feels like a walk upon a razor's edge—life resembles a flickering candle, vulnerable to gusts of chaos. The fragility of safety and the absence of certainty have rendered this era overwhelmingly perilous.

Yet amid such turbulence, a resilient whisper remains—*a Divine Continuity* that persists beneath the surface of chaos.

## Our Constant Companion

Life endures through death, light through darkness, hope through misery, and resilience through repeated failure. These very paradoxes are not accidents but hints of a deeper rhythm. To discern the sacred thread that runs through the mundane, we must train ourselves to see *God's Presence*, feel His touch, and recognise His providence—not merely in rare or spectacular incidents, but in everyday events and encounters. This deeper perception transforms how we interpret even the simplest occurrences and invites us to reframe what we call miracles.

Miracles are not limited to infrequent, seemingly inexplicable phenomena. We are constantly surrounded by an abundance of miracles amongst things that occur frequently and regularly. Each dawn that bathes the earth in light is a miracle. Each breath that sustains life, each heartbeat that keeps us alive, is a miracle. The tender bond of love between two beings is as wondrous as any extraordinary phenomenon.

As an anonymous sage profoundly observed:

*"Miracles often lie even in the simple moments where we find ourselves safely gathered, though every conceivable hindrance could have prevented our meeting. Yet we are brought together unharmed—it is a testament to Divine intervention and protection."*

What lends an event its miraculous nature is not merely its evident *how*, but its profound *why*—the mystery it holds, the awe it inspires, and the Spiritual sensitivity through which it is perceived.

To see God only in thunderous storms, raging cyclones, or seismic upheavals is to make Him an occasional spectacle—admired fleetingly and then forgotten. Such thinking distances Him, rendering Him an occasional visitor rather than an abiding companion.

Craving for the unusual and sensational gives rise to an abnormal state of mind, unrooted in the wisdom of common sense.

The *Mind*, in its pursuit of the extraordinary, often indulges in fancies, illusions, and hallucinatory delights. A Spiritual View is a *Supersense.* It does not negate but exceeds common sense.

If God is to be our constant companion, friend, guide, and guardian—if we are to grow in His image—we should bring Him from the heaven of perfection to our earth of limitations.

## Deepening Bonds with the Divine

These reflections, though inspiring, prompt a direct and challenging question: *How does one realise God in life?*

To embark on this *Path*, we must shun doubt, despair, fear, and inconsistency. Instead, we must cultivate trust, confidence, enthusiasm, and sincerity. A cheerful spirit, a loving disposition towards life and its intricacies, and a forgiving nature are essential companions on this journey. Wisdom also demands that we honour essential values over trivial distractions. The virtues we aspire to are not easily attained—for the intent to achieve them must be bound by profound sincerity.

Yet *sincerity* is not as simple as it seems. A keen self-analysis reveals that artificiality can hide beneath the show of sincerity. A courteous smile is easy to offer, but a genuine smile—the expression of wholehearted cheerfulness—is rare. Formal sympathy may be abundant, but heartfelt empathy—where we genuinely partake in the joys and sorrows of others—is a rarity.

*True virtue*, admired not for its reward but for its inherent nobility, is indispensable. Virtue, recognised wherever it appears, forms the bedrock of a *Godly Life*.

Without qualifying ourselves with these essential requisites, it is idle to hope to attain God or live a *Godly Life*. Meditation or yogic practices performed in brief intervals cannot substitute for a life consciously attuned to the *Divine*. If there is no conscious effort to turn the whole life into *God-Realisation*, what is gained in sincere meditation may be undone by living the remainder of the day in contradiction to that ideal.

Impressive terminology, speculative subtlety, and intellectual finesse offer little in the pursuit of *Ultimate Realisation*. God must be brought into factual life—life that is purified, sanctified, and surrendered. The aspirant must no longer be content with abstract belief; he must seek direct contact with God.

But for such contact to emerge, the barriers within must be seen for what they are—subtle veils that obscure clarity.

Although the *Sadhak* may believe in God and even associate certain actions and experiences with Him, a veil remains that obstructs clear vision. This curtain must be removed or rendered transparent. The question then arises: *How may this be achieved?*

## Growing in Faith

The path of the *Sadhak* begins with belief—fragile and tentative, yet potent enough to set the Soul on its journey towards the Divine. The *Sadhak* reflects, *"Though I do not see Him, He sees me. I am unable to hear His whispers, but He listens to my Prayers and responds to them through actions and the fruits of my efforts. I think of Him rarely; He thinks of me always."*

When belief flowers into Faith and sincerity into earnestness, the Sadhak realises that God is not something to be added to life, but is already the thread woven through its fabric.

Household chores, however simple, become sanctified—as though one were preparing a temple for the Divine. Bathing is no longer routine but a quiet act of cleansing, purifying both body and Soul. Each meal is not mere sustenance but a sacred gift of Nature, received with reverence. Moved by gratitude, the Sadhak asks, *'How am I worthy of such care? How may I ever return such boundless Grace?'*

This sacred perspective permeates every aspect of life. Work ceases to be a mundane obligation and becomes a Divine service offered to God, the Eternal Master. Family and community are no longer mere human connections; they are visible manifestations of the invisible God. Success and failure, joy and sorrow, honour and humiliation—each becomes a Divine instrument for Spiritual evolution, a call to grow, purify, and awaken. The *Sadhak* soon realises that he was chosen for God's work and that he must do this work to the best of his ability, worthy of Him and His trust.

He realises that he is a devoted servant in *God's vineyard* or a loyal soldier in His *army.* He is intended by God to purify and beautify life, to fight evil and misery, to serve suffering humanity, and to establish Divine order through the work allotted to him.

His family, society, and all human interactions become opportunities for him to connect with God. Nature reveals the Divine play; the universe becomes a living garden, and every leaf a page from God's scripture.

Even the most unendurable difficulties do not shake the *Sadhak's* Faith, for he grows in certainty that the Omniscient God knows what is happening to him and that He will always remain by his side, sharing his sufferings and strengthening him during the ordeal. The *Sadhak* does not lose his Faith even in dismal situations. He says, with a knowing smile, *"If it is His will that I should perish, let it be so in His immediate Presence. What greater boon is there than to fulfil His wish?"*

## Experiencing the Oneness

As the bond with the unseen God deepens, the *Sadhak* feels a sense of certainty in his belonging. *"He is mine. I am His. No power can sever this bond."* This marks the first stage of *Tasyai Vaham*—an inner flowering of calm, strength, and humility born of Divine attachment. But for this bond to truly anchor itself in experience, the illusion of separation must entirely be dispelled.

हिरण्मयेन पात्रेण सत्यस्यापिहितं मुखम्।
तत्त्वं पूषन्नपावृणु सत्यधर्माय दृष्टये॥

*The face of Truth is hidden by a golden blaze, O Sun, O luminous guardian of the ways–withdraw thy radiant veil, let the Light break free, that one who walks in Truth may behold and see. -Verse 15: Isha Upanishad.*

The curtain or the Golden Lid hiding God is not outside the devotee; it is within him. Through Faith, sincerity, and strength of aspiration, and by constantly associating events with God, the absent God becomes the present God, and the distant God becomes the near. *He* becomes *Thou.* God in the third person becomes God in the second person. The emotional bond strengthens, and the veil begins to thin—or perhaps vanish altogether.

As closeness deepens, so does affection. The dear becomes near, and the near becomes dearer still. Gradually, the Divine becomes the sole, All-Absorbing Reality. Nature appears anew—Intelligence becomes visible in material things, and God's Presence is perceived in every detail.

## The Seen and Unseen Divine

The devotee sees the smiling face of God in flowers and His Luminous Presence in the sun and moon. The rustling of leaves, murmuring of streams, the roar of the ocean, whispers of breeze, birdsong, cries of animals—even the hum of insects—all seem infused with His voice. The universe vibrates with Divine energy. Every sound, sight, fragrance, and sensation becomes a gateway to Omnipresence. The devotee no longer seeks to see God, for God reveals Himself spontaneously.

This is the stage where belief transforms into direct experience. The world is no longer an illusion, but a manifestation of the Divine. The Sadhak's mind is now so attuned to God that even the most mundane objects and actions take on sacred significance. Life ceases to be ordinary—it turns Transparent, Luminous, infused with Presence. His entire existence becomes a fluid dialogue with the Infinite. Every thought is steeped in reverence, every breath becomes Worship, every movement a form of Prayer. The dichotomy between the devotee and God dissolves—not intellectually, nor metaphorically, but through direct Spiritual experience. The devotee no longer contemplates unity; he lives it.

## The Final Stage: Living the Realisation

As the journey approaches fulfilment, the sense of individual identity begins to fade and merge into singular awareness. The devotee's consciousness expands, and he perceives that the same Divine essence animating his being pervades all existence. The ancient declarations *"Tat Tvam Asi" (That Thou Art) and "Aham Brahmasmi" (I am Brahman)* are no longer scriptural teachings—they have become inner certainties. Separation vanishes. This is not absorption into abstraction—it is awakening into totality.

## Jivanmukti

This state of union is the ultimate stage of Realisation. It is not merely intellectual understanding or emotional attachment, but a direct, lived experience of being one with the Divine. The devotee transcends the limitations of the mind and body and enters a state of pure Consciousness, where there is no distinction between the knower, the known, and the knowledge.

Pleasure and pain, gain and loss, life and death no longer bind or distract. He remains rooted in the Eternal, untouched by the fluctuations of the phenomenal world. In this state of Union, the *Sadhak* no longer seeks God—for he abides in God. Thought, Word, and Deed emerge not from effort, but from the natural overflow of *Divine Clarity. He lives in the world yet is not of the world.* Like the lotus untouched by water, he remains immersed yet unaffected. His life becomes a spontaneous offering—each action performed without attachment; each interaction steeped in compassion.

The final stage of Realisation is not a conclusion—it is an inception.

The *Sadhak*, now fully Realised, lives as a *Jivanmukta*—a *Liberated Soul* abiding in the body, who does not withdraw from the world but engages with it more fully, with a heightened sense of purpose and responsibility. He has attained the supreme goal of Life—Union with the Divine. He has realised his true Nature as the Eternal, infinite Self, beyond all limitations of time, space, and causality. He lives in the perpetual awareness of this Truth, fully immersed in the Divine, yet fully present in the world.

Thus, navigating life with a profound sense of inner peace and joy, his heart overflowing with love for all beings, he becomes a beacon of light and inspiration for others, guiding them on their own Spiritual journeys. His very presence radiates the peace and bliss of Divine Realisation, uplifting all who come into contact with him.

This is the ultimate stage of Realisation—the culmination of the Spiritual Journey that transcends all concepts and descriptions. It is the fulfilment of the *Soul's* deepest longing and the Realisation of its highest potential. The *Sadhak* has come home to his true Self—and in this state of Divine union, he abides forever in perfect peace, bliss, and freedom.

## Beyond Stages

The stages of Realisation are not rigid or linear; they may overlap, and the journey may involve moving back and forth between different phases. Each individual's Spiritual path is unique, shaped by their own temperament, experience, and the *Divine Grace* that guides them. However, the essence of the journey remains unchanged—moving from Ignorance to Knowledge, from Separation to Union, and from the Limited Self to the Infinite Divine.

Sincerity, Faith, and Perseverance are the traveller's tools. With a true Guru's guidance and Divine Grace as a compass, the *Sadhak* inevitably reaches the summit. In this summit, there is just silence. *And in that silence—everything.*

This is the Path of Realisation, the *Journey of the Soul*, and the ultimate fulfilment of Human Life. Each of us is destined to undertake this journey—and in it, we find our True Home in the Eternal embrace of the Divine.

# CHAPTER 17

# The Root of Fear

An honest examination of our thoughts and feelings reveals a startling yet fundamental truth—the fear of death, which lies at the root of many of our actions. This weight of dread often compels us to forgo righteous choices or surrender to errant ones. Were this singular fear overcome, man would find himself liberated from nearly all anxiety and sorrow.

The Vedic rishi, with profound wisdom, declares:

*'O children of Immortality! Listen, Listen! I have seen the Supreme Person, resplendent in His Self-Luminosity, shining on the other shore of ignorance. Those who desire to cross the ocean of death must realise Him. There is no other way to transcend the vast sea of mortality.'*

This proclamation carries not just poetic grandeur but Eternal relevance. The sage recognises that the fear of death is an immense force—one that stands between man and the fulfilment he seeks, obstructing his Spiritual ascent. Yet within this utterance breathes an enduring conviction: that man is inherently Immortal. His words transcend boundaries of time and geography; they speak to all of Humanity.

## Inner Ignorance

In our day-to-day existence, we often find ourselves living on the surface of life, unaware of the deeper forces at work beneath. We remain oblivious to the subtle influences from the world around us, the environment of consciousness that affects our thoughts, feelings, and actions. Rarely do we touch the hidden depths of our own being, and even less often do we perceive the grand design of *Super-Consciousness* shaping our *Journey.*

Our daily routines, vocations, and responsibilities often keep us so engrossed in the issues of the moment that we lose sight of Life's true aim. In this manner, we drift through existence, side-tracked by momentary concerns, disconnected from the *sacred centre* of our being.

Then, abruptly, death strikes, and a loved one vanishes from this plane. The event shakes us to our roots, shattering our routines and notions of permanence. Questions arise: "*What is this? Why is this? Is this the only truth?*"

In such moments of piercing vulnerability, it is not analysis but surrender that opens the way. We must turn humbly to the Lord of Life, asking for guidance, Illumination, and Grace—to receive the Inner Wisdom needed to understand this ultimate mystery.

## Death: The Reality

Death, as ancient as life itself, remains an unsolved enigma—crossing cultures, eras, and intellects. It makes no distinction: rich or poor, scholar or illiterate, monarch or mendicant, saint or transgressor—all are equal before its threshold.

Physicians who save others stand powerless before their own hour. Warriors who stained battlefields with blood could not hold back the hovering death. Prophets reputed to raise the dead ultimately surrendered to their own departure.

Poets have sung its lament, scientists have analysed its patterns, philosophers have proposed meanings—but death defies full comprehension. Rather than treating it as an abstraction, we must examine its influence—how it confronts us, and how we may respond with Spiritual clarity.

Aristotle observed that the purpose of tragedy in drama is the purification of the emotions of its audience. If theatrical sorrow can refine us, real-life tragedy, especially the loss of life, provokes a far deeper transformation. This concept is referred to in the *Vedantic* tradition as *Chitta Shuddhi*, the purification of the Mind or Consciousness.

As Sri Aurobindo reminds us:

*"The Universe is not built with random bricks of chance. A blind God is not Destiny's architect. A conscious power has drawn the plan of Life; there is meaning in every curve and line."*

Indeed, sorrows often serve as catalysts for Spiritual growth, much more so than the fleeting joys of life. And among sorrows, none purifies like death. It pierces illusions, leaving only stark truths.

After encountering loss, one may be drawn inward—to sainthood, philanthropy, or philosophical reflection. Grief unsettles but also elevates. Though the ways of heaven may seem inscrutable, and fate at times unjust, it is through these trials that Faith and Patience are tempered and forged.

## The Paradox of Death

In the *Mahabharata*, Yudhishthira is asked, 'What is the most astonishing phenomenon?' His reply is timeless: 'Death.'

Why? It is common knowledge that all who are born are destined to die. Plants die, animals die, and human beings die. *'Jaatasya maranam dhruvam'*—the death of that which is born is certain. Death hovers around us constantly, yet we live our lives largely oblivious to it.

No one truly believes their own death is near, even when it stands silently before them. This paradox—our grasp of death intellectually while denying it emotionally—eludes logic and psychology alike. This contradiction is not resolved by conditioning ourselves to accept death emotionally, but by recognising the deeper truth of Immortality that is embedded in our unconscious mind.

Man does not die, for his Soul is Eternal. This is why we instinctively deny death despite overwhelming evidence to the contrary. Just as the Earth's rotation creates the illusion that the sun is moving, so too does our perceptual understanding confuse the perishable body with the imperishable Soul.

The Vedic wisdom proclaims:

*'If God is Eternal, His child is Eternal, too. If Paramaathman is forever, its offshoot, the Jeevathman, too, is forever. The Jeevathman, or the individual, shares in the Immortality of the Paramaathman—the Supreme Soul.'*

The Soul abides in God—not as a fleeting emanation, but as an Eternal Presence, akin to fragrance belonging to the flower and light to the flame. Death is not cessation—it is transition. The Soul journeys onward, beyond the dissolution of form, sustained in the timeless embrace of the Divine.

## Mourning the Departed

Our grief often arises because we identify our loved ones solely with their physical bodies. When their form disappears into flame or earth, we are left dazed, unable to accept the shift. We cling to the impermanent and suffer when impermanence asserts itself.

Unless we learn the grace of letting go consciously, we will be forced to surrender painfully under strain. If we do not welcome this truth as a guest, it will arrive as a conqueror and claim everything we hold dear.

Are we not constantly shedding our physical selves—our cells renewing, bodies transforming? Every seven years, our form is entirely renewed. So, when death arrives, it is not an end, but a passage into invisibility. The essence persists. Invisible forces, after all, govern visible matter, and often last longer than their manifestations.

Recovery from bereavement begins by distinguishing *form* from *substance, vessel* from *essence.* Our attachment should shift from the form to the content within the form. We must then train our perception to recognise the same Divine content in changing forms —varied yet sharing a common essence. By embracing this approach, it becomes possible to overcome the illusory sense of separation that death seems to impose.

## Coping with Bereavement

Those who shared deep bonds with the departed *can* experience their subtle presence. They can connect with the departed through the eye of Faith and the ear of Conscience. Just as physical distance doesn't sever relationships between those living continents apart, neither does bodily absence nullify the *Soul's* connection. Faith, Hope, and Spiritual Sensitivity keep love alive.

This is not hallucinatory, but a natural psychological experience. What we see in dreams—vivid and profound—is not seen with eyes, but with the inner Self. Similarly, it is the *Soul* that feels the presence of the departed, independent of physical sight.

We do not mourn the loss of what we never knew. What we lament is the absence of one with whom we shared a deep bond. Yet, all that we knew of the departed—their qualities, our relationship, our experiences—remains intact within us. The best of them, what they revealed to us and brought into our lives, continues to dwell within our hearts. Though outward interaction is no longer possible, inward communion remains ever attainable.

Whenever the heart longs for the nearness of the departed, we may turn inward in reverent remembrance. Through memory, imagination, and pure emotion, the presence of those we love can be felt again—not selfishly, but with gratitude. It is akin to speaking to a distant friend over the phone: the gestures, the smiles, and the connection endure, though the physical form is absent.

We must understand that all the good that was revealed in them belongs to God. It was God who disclosed Himself through their lives, and His presence abides behind their actions. With this recognition, we find solace and peace, knowing that they are still with us.

By believing in their Spiritual presence, drawing strength from their memory, and fulfilling their noble aspirations, we carry forward their legacy. Their essence is assimilated and immortalised through our actions. Thus they live on—not in name alone, but in the eternal continuity of the Spirit.

# CHAPTER 18

# Whither Are We Drifting?

A schoolteacher once entered the classroom holding the *world map* to deliver a lesson in Moral Science. The students were puzzled—why bring a world map for such a subject? The teacher hung the map on the wall and posed a question:

*"Imagine I tear this map into pieces—not into neat, geometric shapes but irregular fragments—and you are tasked with piecing it back together perfectly. Who among you can do it?"*

The class, full of bright and devoted students, hesitated. Looking at the maze of lines and curves on the map, they responded in unison: *"Impossible!"*

One girl rose, and with the teacher's permission, walked up to the map. She turned it over, examined the reverse, and, after a moment of contemplation, returned to her seat. With quiet confidence, she declared she could complete the task. The teacher asked how.

*"On the reverse side of the world map is the figure of a human being. If I reconstruct the human figure first—with fewer lines and simpler contours—the world map will automatically come together,"* she explained.

The teacher and students were astonished. Her insight revealed a profound truth.

## Man—and the World

This example offers a vital lesson—not only for us, but also for those entrusted with shaping humanity's fate. The relationship between man and the world mirrors the torn map: our outer disorder reflects inner fragmentation. To mend the world, we must first understand and restore human nature.

What is a *problem*, after all? Does it arise purely from external circumstances? We see that the same situation affects different people in diverse ways. Even under one roof, family members face varied challenges—the concerns of the working differ from those of the dependent; the aged from the young; the married from the unmarried. Even shared experiences carry different weights in each mind.

To say *Life* gives us problems is a misnomer. Life offers *situations*—it is the *mind* that interprets these as problems. Each person responds differently, and even within the same individual, reactions may vary over time. A problem is simply a disharmony in the Mind's response—factual when practical, conceptual when psychological. It is the dynamic interplay of situation and inner state.

This leads us to a deeper inquiry—if individual interpretation creates problems, then the collective turmoil of this world must reflect a shared inner conflict.

## The Root of All Problems

The world has tried many remedies for various situations, including ecological responsibility, disarmament, population control, and simplified living. These are noble pursuits, yet they often address symptoms rather than causes. Once resolved on one front, problems re-emerge elsewhere.

Despite human brilliance, ingenuity, and tireless effort, difficulties persist—becoming increasingly elusive. The root does not lie in policy or politics, but in the person. This is the uncomfortable truth that history repeatedly tells us.

Political philosophers lament the shortcomings of monarchy, dictatorship, and even democracy. However, the bitter truth remains that *systems* fail because *humans* fail. The real crisis is not merely that man faces problems, but that his fragmented nature perpetuates them.

Without a Moral, Mental, and Spiritual renewal, no external reform can truly succeed.

Science has lifted man to celestial realms—he has reached the Moon, touched Mars—but cannot yet bridge the far shorter distance to a neighbour's heart. Fear, suspicion, and discord still sever the human bond. Thus, when Humanity loses its moral and Spiritual compass, even the finest governance fails to bring peace.

True progress demands not that machinery be reshuffled but consciousness be transformed. Every great epoch in civilisation emerged from an inner revolution—a refusal to stagnate, a thirst for idealism, a call toward self-renewal.

And if man himself is the source, then only a transformation of his consciousness can offer true resolution.

## Humanism as the Remedy

Humanism—goodness in its most active and luminous form—is the sovereign remedy for Humanity's afflictions. The difference between a saint and a sinner lies only in the degree to which goodness manifests.

It is goodness that confers dignity, guides talent, gives meaning to instinct, and defines purpose. It is not passivity, nor mere absence of vice—it is a positive, dynamic, and righteous force. Among all virtues, goodness stands nearest to Godliness. It rests upon two pillars: reverence for truth and consideration for others. This is the essence of Humanism.

But why do people struggle to be good? Why do noble actions seem so difficult to uphold? The obstacles are rooted in fear and selfishness. Only when one realises that harming others is harming oneself—and that all are bound together in *Eternal unity*—can these barriers dissolve.

Selfless goodness becomes possible when man discovers he is not a transient form, but an indestructible essence, forever linked to Humanity.

The frameworks of culture, civilisation, and religion were conceived—not merely to organise society, but to awaken the timeless Self, to honour the indestructible essence within man.

## The Aim of Culture, Civilisation and Religion

The aim of all culture, the promise of civilisation, the discipline of every Spiritual teaching, is to awaken human strength by revealing man's highest potential.

We are not merely thinking animals—we are Eternal beings, inherently interconnected. True civilisation is not *ornamentation* but *Illumination.*

Evolution through matter, life, and mind marks the journey toward realising our Divine Nature.

Humanism surpasses all racial, national, and geographical divisions. It is the meeting point of all religions, the convergence of Spiritual intention. The diversity of religious forms is the expression of the same fundamental truth and the blossoming of one Eternal seed.

Why then has religion, meant to unify and uplift, often become a force that divides and demeans? Why this troubling anomaly and painful paradox?

The answer lies in misplaced focus—Ritual over Realisation, Form over Essence. More dangerous still is religious bigotry, which leads us away from one another and traps us in self-defined compartments of *"exclusive truth"*.

Truth may be approached in three distinct ways. The first says, *"This is true,"* and reflects a spirit of affirmation without exclusion. It honours one's own insight or tradition while remaining open to the possibility that others, too, may glimpse the Infinite through different windows. The second declares, *"This alone is not true."* Though it may arise from a sincere quest for authenticity, it risks becoming reactionary—dismissing a tradition without full understanding, and sometimes falling into cynicism or spiritual isolation. The third asserts, *"This alone is true,"* and here lies the real seed of fanaticism. It confines Truth to a single formulation, often elevating dogma above experience, and restricts brotherhood to creed.

Genuine Spiritual brotherhood transcends identity—it embraces Humanity. It recognises that while Truth is One, its expressions are many. Intolerance often arises from impatience, which may mask insecurity. It corrupts devotion, just as jealousy warps love. Religion must return to its essence—inner freedom, honesty, and communion. One must be free to accept or reject scriptures and teachers, guided by reason, conscience, and intuition. This principle of Spiritual autonomy aligns with the deeper teachings of all great Faiths, though it may differ from popular beliefs and practices.

Religious institutions must lead not by doctrine but by example. A true seeker's life should reflect integrity and a spirit of helpfulness. Daily communion with God nourishes the *Soul.* The seeker's home must become a mission house, where prayer and celebration honour the Divine presence and sanctity, becoming the pulse of family life.

When we realise that God reveals Himself through the wonders of the Universe, the splendours of Nature, and the stirring events of our lives, our day-to-day lives become Spiritual endeavours, and every moment of awe, surprise, or deep emotion becomes a communion with the Divine.

Every experience—joy or sorrow, trivial or significant—is an invitation to refine the inner Self, to cast away base tendencies, and to rise in the image of the Divine.

Whether we widen our perspectives, soften our judgments, or awaken our inner strength, each experience carries Spiritual meaning when touched by reverence.

## Union with the Divine

In harmony with God, we find fulfilment; out of tune, we become barren—like a drop of water separated from the ocean. United, the drop partakes of the ocean's vastness. Separated, it vanishes.

God, the Divine charioteer of our Journey, guides us through difficulty and invites us to face life with dignity and joy.

Here is a contextual Prayer to complete this reflection:

*"O Divine Source of Grace and Truth, we bow in gratitude for the revelations Thou hast bestowed, guiding us towards an era where Human values transcend creeds and divisions.*

*In Thy Eternal Unity, we find our connection, for we, Thy children, are threads woven into the fabric of Thy boundless Self.*

*Grant us the strength to uphold this sacred gift—a beacon to light our path and inspire those who journey alongside us. Recharge our spirits with Thy presence, fortify our wills, and transform our weakness into strength so that we may remain steadfast in truth and righteousness.*

*May we seek Thee daily, finding joy in harmony, peace, and love. Teach us to walk in unity, trusting Thy guidance, and may our lives reflect Thy Light, bringing hope and strength to all."*

# CHAPTER 19

# The Journey Home

At the close of our journey, we arrive at Life itself—the silent, unseen thread binding all that we have touched, pondered, and experienced. We have sought the essence of divinity, reflected on the foundations of Faith, faced the shadow of death, and glimpsed into the Eternal. Now, we stand before the profound mystery of living—not as a simple act, but as an expression of existence in its totality—a journey of being, becoming, and ultimately dissolving into a vastness beyond the self. In this sacred unfolding, to live well, and to make Life a true art, is to embody timeless truths in each moment—to weave the wisdom of the Eternal into the humble fabric of each day.

## The Mystery of Life

What is this mystery that we call *Life*—elusive, unseen, yet undeniably present? However we attempt to define it, we capture only a fragment, an aspect. A complete understanding remains beyond our grasp. There is in Life an abiding element of the unknown—a quiet profundity that calls to us but resists full explanation. We are vaguely aware of what stirs in the hidden regions of consciousness—the seat of higher forces; and in the deeper recesses of the psyche, where subtle influences shape our thoughts and will. Life moves in cycles and seasons, revealing itself in its varied dramas of conflict and beauty, in its passages of joy and sorrow, and in its stories of aspiration and fall. The pattern of Life's journey—its origin, its purpose, its ultimate goal—is all marked by paradoxes.

What, then, is Life to be compared with? By what standards might it be measured? We ascribe goodness to one object, beauty to another, usefulness here, and value there. But how are we to measure Life itself—its inherent goodness, its sacred beauty, its value as the vessel for our noblest aspirations? All that we praise as beautiful or useful derives its significance from *Life*. Apart from *Life*, such terms are hollow, abstractions without living substance.

Life is not a punishment or a consequence of past error, nor a prison from which we are meant to escape. It is a *gift*—a radiant offering of joy from the Infinite. If Truth is the essence, and Wisdom its guide, then Love is its source—the power that kindled *Creation*.

The *Upanishads* proclaim:

*'Out of joy are we born; by joy, we are sustained, and unto joy, we return.'*

This joy, when touched, becomes love; and in love, life finds its deepest expression. Love is both the impetus of life and its consummation. Without *love*, life is barren; without *life*, love remains only potential. In this union, the mystery of life is revealed—and through living fully, we draw nearer to the quiet truths of our being.

## Cultivating the Ultimate Art

To live fully is to embody this Divine artistry in our daily lives, with God as the Master Artist whose hand shapes every colour, every line, every contour of experience.

To live well is to walk the inner path with grace—a journey shaped by courage, patience, humour, fortitude, self-trust, and a reverent fidelity to Truth. Life does not always yield to our plans, yet we must dream and act. Its rhythm may diverge from our expectations, yet we must strive and endure. No effort is excessive, and no precaution is misplaced, yet our effort alone does not govern life's unfolding. The journey home is not a conquest, but a surrender—an alignment of our Will with a Higher Law that silently shapes our destinies, both individual and collective.

In this harmony, the Soul finds freedom—not through control, but through trust. Trust in the Hidden Wisdom that silently guides each unfolding, and recognition that beyond all human reckoning, a Higher Intelligence is ever at work.

To realise and manifest this harmony in our lives, the *Upanishadic* sages have taught that the aim of life is God-Realisation—to find the Divine within the world, within ourselves, and to reveal Him through our living.

The Earth exists for the creatures living upon it; the creatures fulfil their purpose in service to the planet. The Self-Luminous, Immortal person hidden in the Consciousness of Earth and the Soul of Humanity is the same. He is the Supreme Being, Brahma, the Source and culmination of all.

The ultimate purpose of life is the Spiritual perfection of man—the Truth that alone illuminates every experience. For, behind each event and unfolding moment, there lies intention, not accident, but shaped by a Conscious Power that has drawn the blueprint of his destiny.

## The Boundless Nature

From time immemorial, seekers have turned to Nature not as a backdrop for human life but as the very garment of the Divine. The rivers and forests, the mountains and skies, were not seen as mute scenery but as living presences, revealing the Infinite in countless forms. The sages discerned in every breeze the breath of the Spirit, in every ray of light the touch of Grace. They did not stand apart from Nature as its masters, but entered into its intimacy as children of the Eternal Mother.

The saint-poet Bhartruhari, at the twilight of his life, gave voice to this reverence:

*"O Mother Earth, Air our grandsire, Light our friend, Water our kin, Brother Sky—accept my gratitude. With this wisdom, I take refuge in the Supreme Person—Parabrahma."*

Such a vision does not belong to any one culture or age; it is the Universal recognition that Life is a web of relationships, woven together by the threads of the Spirit. To live in harmony with Nature is not to glorify a particular past, but to remember the timeless Truth: that communion with the elements is communion with the Eternal, and to wound Nature is to estrange ourselves from God. Modern civilisation, with all its wonders, need not be rejected; but this deeper awareness must illumine it, lest abundance close our eyes to simplicity, or power sever us from reverence.

When life is lived as a partnership with the Spirit that breathes through all, then even the smallest act—drawing water, tending a garden, walking beneath the stars—becomes worship. Nature, thus embraced, becomes the very path on which we walk the Journey Home.

## Inner Harmony

True harmony is not attained by seeking outward gains, but by inward becoming. Renunciation, then, is not simply an act—it is a shift in consciousness. Just as we appreciate the beauty of a river, not by being swept in its current but by observing from the shore, we also experience life's *Truth* from a place of *Inner Stillness.*

True *Spiritual* insight enables us to transcend the divisions of desire and possession, revealing the unity that underlies all existence. In that revelation, beauty relinquishes its need for ownership—like dawn offering light without condition, the sun and stars unveil their splendour to hearts unbarred, radiant in their seeking.

Rabindranath Tagore observed:

*"Beauty is the ideal of perfect harmony in the Universal Being; Truth is comprehension of the Universal Mind. In our sense of Truth, we recognise Law; in Beauty, we realise Harmony. When we perceive Law in our moral nature, we attain mastery and become free. When we feel Harmony in the Soul, Beauty expresses as goodness and love—moving toward the Infinite."*

The sages, both idealistic and realistic, did not ignore the realities of life; instead, they proposed a path of integrated existence—embracing learning, family life, gradual detachment, and ultimately, final renunciation. Each phase invites a fuller expression of self, drawing life closer to its Spiritual purpose.

## The Four Stages of Life

Like the course of a single day, life unfolds in stages. *Brahmacharya* is the dawn—learning and discipline shape the youth. *Grihastha* follows: the householder's life of love, duty, and self-sacrifice. The home becomes the sacred fireplace of shared experience, responsibility, and growth. In *Vanaprastha*, one gradually steps back, passing the torch to the next generation, and learning the quiet wisdom of detachment. Finally comes *Sanyasa*, a complete withdrawal from worldly duties, devoting oneself solely to the realisation of God and to the service of others.

The Soul's pilgrimage through the stages of life is not a wandering without a destination. Each step—whether of striving, struggle, or surrender—is but a movement towards the same horizon. What we seek in knowledge, in love, in power, or in beauty is finally the embrace of the Eternal. To recognise this is to discover that the true end of the journey is also its beginning: to return to the Source from which we came, enriched by experience, yet purified of illusion.

## A Vision of True Fulfilment

From the playful wonder of childhood to the resolute striving of youth, from the steadied responsibility of adulthood to the quiet withdrawal of contemplative age—life moves not merely through time, but through revelation.

Each stage is more than a season—it is an unveiling. The child's joy glimpses the mystery, the youth's fire seeks it, the adult shelters it, and the sage watches it emerge without effort. These phases are not ladders to climb but circles to enter—each drawing us closer to the centre where *Truth* waits in silence.

Fulfilment, then, is not something we build—but something we uncover. It is not earned through striving, nor postponed until later years. It is glimpsed in moments when time softens and Presence widens. The Eternal is not a place beyond—it is the quiet pulse within.

What once dazzled now hums. What once evoked longing now offers peace. What once seemed distant now feels near. Meaning does not declare itself—it dawns slowly, like light through mist. And we, in our ultimate step, do not arrive—we return. Gently. Wordlessly.

In the stillness between moments
In the silence between thoughts
In the gaze that neither seeks nor escapes
*The Eternal dawns*

ॐ तत् सत्

# Glossary of Sanskrit Terms

## A Companion to Glimpses of the Eternal

*This glossary presents the Sanskrit terms found throughout the book, offering their meanings and contextual usage—intended not only to clarify, but to invite reflection. Arising from the Upanishadic and Vedic tradition, these words do not seek to define the Divine, but to point toward it. They are vessels of meaning, shaped by centuries of spiritual inquiry and contemplative insight.*

Advaita: अद्वैत

Meaning: Non-duality; the philosophy that all is One, without a second.

Context: Appears in Chapter 7 (Brahma Stotram) and Chapter 8 (The Upanishadic Prayer), where the seeker is invited to transcend duality and realise the indivisible Unity of Existence.

Reflection: In Advaita, the river and the sea are not two—they are one in flow and essence. The seeker does not merge with God; he awakens to the truth that he was never separate.

Aham Brahmasmi: अहं ब्रह्मास्मि

Meaning: "I am Brahman," a Mahavakya affirming unity with the Absolute.

Context: Chapters 16 and 19. In the final stages of Realisation, the Sadhak feels certain that he is not separate from the Divine and proclaims he is none other than Brahman.

Reflection: Not a proclamation of ego, but a dissolution of it. The wave realises it is the ocean.

Artha: अर्थ

Meaning: Material prosperity; one of the four aims of life (Chaturvidha Purushartha).

Context: Discussed in Chapters 5 and 15, where Artha is seen as necessary but must be guided by Dharma and oriented toward Moksha.

Reflection: When wealth serves wisdom, it becomes a sacred thing. When it serves the ego, it becomes a form of bondage.

Asato Ma Sad Gamaya: असतो मा सद्गमय

Meaning: Lead me from the unreal to the Real.

Context: Chapter 8 (The Upanishadic Prayer). Unreal is not taken here as non-existent, but a fragmented reality, which appears as the Whole. The Sadhak wishes not just to escape from this illusion, but to be rooted in the Truth.

Reflection: A prayer for discernment—to move from illusion to Truth, from shadow to substance.

Astika: आस्तिक

Meaning: One who affirms the authority of the Vedas; commonly understood as a theist.

Context: Explored in Chapter 5 (*Theism vs Atheism*), where the term is redefined beyond mere belief into a deeper affirmation of spiritual principles.

Reflection: True Astika is not one who believes in God, but one who lives in alignment with the Eternal.

Atman: आत्मा

Meaning: The innermost Self—unborn, undying, and indivisible.

Context: Central to Chapters 3, 8, and 15, where the seeker is guided to distinguish the Atman from the ego, body, and mind.

Reflection: To realise the Atman is to awaken to one's true nature beyond form and thought.

Avidya: अविद्या

Meaning: Spiritual ignorance; the veil that obscures true knowledge.

Context: Appears in Chapters 8 and 12, where the seeker is urged to transcend Avidya through discrimination and inner illumination.

Reflection: Like clouds before the sun—it hides, but does not destroy. The sun of Truth remains untouched.

Aviraavirma Edhi: आविराविर्म एधि

Meaning: *"Reveal Thyself to me"*; a prayer from the Aitareya Upanishad.

Context: Featured in Chapter 8 (*The Upanishadic Prayer*), as the seeker's plea for direct Divine revelation—not through intermediaries, but through Presence.

Reflection: The Soul does not seek gifts—it seeks the Giver.

Bhagavad Gita: भगवद्गीता

Meaning: Sacred dialogue between Krishna and Arjuna on duty and liberation.

Context: Explored in Chapter 13 (*Divine Dynamics in the Gita*), where the Gita is presented as a synthesis of Vedantic wisdom and worldly engagement—revealed by Krishna to Arjuna on the battleground. The battleground is not merely a historical setting; it's a metaphor for the inner and outer conflicts that define human life—signalling that life's greatest spiritual teachings often arise amid moral crisis and turmoil.

Reflection: The battlefield becomes a temple. Action becomes worship.

Bhakti: भक्ति

Meaning: Devotion; heartfelt surrender to the Divine.

Context: Woven throughout Chapters 10, 15, and 19, where Bhakti is shown as a path of love, not sentiment—a fire that purifies and uplifts.

Reflection: When love becomes worship, Bhakti is born. It is not attachment—it is offering.

Brahmacharya: ब्रह्मचर्य

Meaning: Stage of disciplined learning; the student's path.

Context: Discussed in Chapter 19 (*The Journey Home*), as the first of the four stages of life, where the seeker prepares the vessel for Divine knowledge.

Reflection: The seed of wisdom is sown in silence and simplicity.

Brahman: ब्रह्मन्

Meaning: The Supreme Reality—formless, infinite, eternal.

Context: Central to Chapters 1, 7, and 15, where Brahman is described as the substratum of all Existence—the One behind the many.

Reflection: That which alone is, beyond thought and name. The silence behind all sound.

Brahma Stotram: ब्रह्म स्तोत्रम्

Meaning: Hymn to Brahman that praises the formless Divine.

Context: Chapter 7 is devoted entirely to this hymn, originally drawn from the *Mahanirvana Tantra*, refined by Devendranath Tagore to reflect Advaitic purity.

Reflection: A song of silence clothed in sacred verse. Not a plea, but a proclamation.

Chaturvidha Purushartha: चतुर्विध पुरुषार्थ

Meaning: The four aims of life—Dharma, Artha, Kama, Moksha.

Context: Discussed in Chapters 5 and 15 as the framework for balanced living.

Reflection: A compass for the Soul's journey—where desire and wealth are guided by righteousness and oriented toward liberation.

Chit: चित्

Meaning: Consciousness; the knowing principle of existence.

Context: Appears in Chapter 7 (*Brahma Stotram*) as one of the attributes of the Divine.

Reflection: Awareness that illumines all experience. The light behind the eye, the knowing behind the thought.

Dakshinam Mukham: दक्षिणं मुखम्

Meaning: "Thy peaceful countenance," from the Svetasvatara Upanishad.

Context: Referenced in Chapter 8 (*The Upanishadic Prayer*) as the seeker's longing for the gentle face of the Divine.

Reflection: The face of serenity that blesses the seeker—not in thunder, but in stillness.

Dharma: धर्म

Meaning: Righteous duty; the moral and spiritual law.

Context: Explored throughout the book, especially in Chapters 5, 13, and 15, as the guiding principle of life.

Reflection: To walk in harmony with one's nature and truth. Dharma is not imposed—it is discovered.

Dwijatva: द्विजत्व

Meaning: "Second birth;" spiritual rebirth into knowledge and duty.

Context: Discussed in Chapter 6 (*Essence of Monotheism*) as part of ceremonial initiation into higher life.

Reflection: When learning becomes a sacred rite, and duty becomes devotion.

Grihastha: गृहस्थ

Meaning: Householder stage; the second of the four stages of life (Ashrama Dharma).

Context: Discussed in Chapter 19 (*The Journey Home*), where worldly responsibilities are not seen as distractions but as opportunities for spiritual growth.

Reflection: In service and care, the Divine is not absent. The home becomes a temple when duty is performed with devotion.

Gunas: गुणाः

Meaning: The three qualities of Nature—Sattva (purity), Rajas (passion), Tamas (inertia).

Context: Explored in Chapters 9 and 12, where the transformation of Gunas is described as a spiritual alchemy.

Reflection: These are not moral judgments but energetic tendencies. The seeker must not suppress them, but transmute them into light.

Jeevatman: जीवात्मन्

Meaning: The individual soul; consciousness veiled by ego and embodiment.

Context: Appears in Chapters 3 and 15, where the Jeevatman is distinguished from the Atman and guided toward Realisation.

Reflection: Like the moon reflected in many waters—one light, many forms.

Jnana: ज्ञान

Meaning: Wisdom; the path of knowledge and discernment.

Context: Woven throughout Chapters 8, 13, and 15, where Jnana is shown as the light that dispels illusion.

Reflection: To see the rope and not the snake—that is Jnana. It is not information, but illumination.

Jivanmukta: जीवन्मुक्त

Meaning: One who is liberated while still in the body.

Context: Referenced in Chapter 15 and Chapter 19, as the ideal of spiritual freedom attained in life.

Reflection: Freedom not from life, but within it. The lotus blooms in the mud, untouched by it.

Kama: काम

Meaning: Desire; emotional and sensual fulfilment.

Context: Discussed in Chapter 5 and Chapter 15, where Kama is acknowledged as part of human nature but must be refined and guided.

Reflection: When purified, even longing becomes luminous. Desire becomes devotion when it seeks the Eternal.

Karma Yoga: कर्मयोग

Meaning: Path of selfless action; work offered without attachment to results.

Context: Central to Chapter 13 (*Divine Dynamics in the Gita*), where Karma Yoga is presented as the way to spiritualise daily life.

Reflection: In doing without grasping, one finds peace. Action becomes offering.

Maya: माया

Meaning: Illusion; the appearance that veils Reality.

Context: Explored in Chapters 8 and 15, where Maya is described as the cosmic play that hides the One behind the many.

Reflection: The dance of forms before the formless. To see through Maya is to awaken.

Moksha: मोक्ष

Meaning: Liberation from bondage, ignorance, and the cycle of birth and death.

Context: Appears in Chapters 15 and 19 as the goal of spiritual life—not escape, but Realisation.

Reflection: The Soul's return to its source, where all dualities dissolve and only Truth remains.

Mrityorma Amritam Gamaya: मृत्योर्मामृतं गमय

Meaning: "Lead me from death to immortality."

Context: Quoted in Chapter 8 (*The Upanishadic Prayer*) as part of the seeker's ascent from fear to freedom.

Reflection: A Brihadaranyaka Upanishad prayer for transcendence, not escape. To die to illusion is to be born into Truth.

Mukti Samaj: मुक्ति समाज

Meaning: "Liberation Society," a monotheistic spiritual congregation.

Context: Referenced in Chapter 6 (*Essence of Monotheism*), where reformist movements are discussed as vehicles of spiritual renewal.

Reflection: Where unity is worshipped and freedom is sought—not in ritual, but in Realisation.

Nyaya: न्याय

Meaning: School of logic and epistemology; one of the six classical Darshanas.

Context: Mentioned in Chapter 5 and Chapter 15, where reason is shown as a tool—not an obstacle—to spiritual insight.

Reflection: Reason as a bridge to Truth. When logic bows to wisdom, it becomes luminous.

Paramatman: परमात्मन्

Meaning: The Universal Self; the Atman in all beings.

Context: Appears in Chapters 3 and 15, where the seeker is guided to see the same Self in all.

Reflection: One light shining through many windows. The Eternal behind every face.

Pathithapavana: पतितपावन

Meaning: Redeemer of the fallen; sanctifier of the erring.

Context: Referenced in Chapter 6, where Divine Grace is shown as inclusive and transformative. God descends to man to uplift him and, in turn, be uplifted.

Reflection: Grace that lifts without judgment. The touch that heals without asking.

Prarthana Samaj: प्रार्थना समाज

Meaning: "Prayer Society," a reformist spiritual movement.

Context: Discussed in Chapter 6 (*Essence of Monotheism*), as part of India's spiritual renaissance.

Reflection: Devotion with clarity, tradition with renewal. A bridge between ancient wisdom and modern aspiration.

Purusha: पुरुष

Meaning: The witnessing Self; the eternal subject behind all experience.

Context: Appears in Chapters 3 and 15, where Purusha is contrasted with Prakriti (Nature).

Reflection: Still, silent, and sovereign. The one who sees but is never seen.

Rajas: रजस्

Meaning: Quality of passion, restlessness, and desire.

Context: Explored in Chapters 9 and 12, where Rajas is shown as the force of movement that must be refined.

Reflection: The fire that moves, but also burns. When harnessed, it becomes dynamic harmony.

Sadhak: साधक

Meaning: Spiritual aspirant; one who walks the path of Sadhana.

Context: Appears in Chapters 11 and 19, where the Sadhak is portrayed not by attainment, but by sincerity.

Reflection: Defined not by arrival, but by longing. The journey itself is sacred.

Sadhana: साधना

Meaning: Spiritual discipline undertaken with sincerity and vigilance.

Context: Chapter 11 (*Sadhana: The Sage's Vigil*) explores Sadhana as the quiet effort that awakens the Soul.

Reflection: Each step, a prayer in motion. The path where aspiration becomes Realisation.

Sankhya: सांख्य

Meaning: Philosophical system of dualism by Sage Kapila.

Context: Mentioned in Chapter 15, where Sankhya is acknowledged as a precursor to Vedanta.

Reflection: Counting the seen to reach the unseen. A ladder from matter to Spirit.

Sanyasa: संन्यास

Meaning: Renunciation; the final stage of spiritual life.

Context: Discussed in Chapter 19 (*The Journey Home*), where Sanyasa is shown not as withdrawal, but as inner freedom.

Reflection: When the world is laid down, the Self rises. Renunciation is not an escape—it is Realisation.

Sat: सत्

Meaning: Existence; pure being.

Context: Appears in Chapter 7 (*Brahma Stotram*) and Chapter 15, as one of the attributes of Brahman.

Reflection: That which never ceases to be. The ground of all that is.

Sattva: सत्त्व

Meaning: Quality of purity and harmony.

Context: Explored in Chapters 9 and 12, where Sattva is shown as the foundation of spiritual aspiration.

Reflection: Sattva leads to inner peace and a centred personality. Among the Gunas, it is the uplifting force that leads to liberation.

Shad-Darsanas: षड्दर्शनाः

Meaning: The six classical schools of Hindu philosophy.

Context: Mentioned in Chapter 15, where each system is acknowledged as a unique lens on Truth.

Reflection: Diverse paths, one destination. The Eternal glimpsed through many windows.

Swadharma: स्वधर्म

Meaning: One's own duty; the law of one's being.

Context: Discussed in Chapters 13 and 15, where Swadharma is shown as the path of authenticity and alignment.

Reflection: To be true to oneself is to honour the Divine. Duty becomes devotion when it flows from the Soul.

Tamas: तमस्

Meaning: Quality of inertia and ignorance.

Context: Appears in Chapters 9 and 12, where Tamas is shown as the shadow that must be transmuted.

Reflection: The darkness that hides, yet invites awakening. When transformed, it becomes poise and depth.

Tamaso Ma Jyotirgamaya: तमसो मा ज्योतिर्गमय

Meaning: Lead me from darkness to light.

Context: Quoted in Chapter 8 (The Upanishadic Prayer), this invocation is part of the seeker's ascent from ignorance to illumination.

Reflection: The journey from confusion to clarity. Light is not given—it is uncovered.

Tat Tvam Asi: तत् त्वम् असि

Meaning: "That Thou Art;" a Mahavakya affirming unity with Brahman.

Context: Referenced in Chapters 16 and 19 as the culmination of the seeker's journey.

Reflection: The whisper of the Eternal in the heart of the seeker. Not a metaphor, but a Realisation.

Upanayana Samskara: उपनयन संस्कार

Meaning: Ceremonial initiation into Vedic learning.

Context: Mentioned in Chapter 6 (Essence of Monotheism), where the rite is described as a symbolic rebirth into spiritual knowledge.

Reflection: A rite of passage into sacred learning. The thread of wisdom is woven into the Soul.

Upanishad: उपनिषद्

Meaning: Scriptures of philosophical inquiry and spiritual insight; the culmination of Vedic wisdom.

Context: Central to Chapter 8 (The Upanishadic Prayer), where verses from Aitareya, Bruhadaranyak, and Svetasvatara Upanishads are invoked.

Reflection: Not taught, but revealed. The Upanishads are not doctrines—they are distilled experience.

Uttara Mimamsa / Vedanta: उत्तर मीमांसा / वेदान्त

Meaning: Philosophical inquiry into Brahman and Self; the "end" of the Vedas.

Context: Discussed in Chapter 15 (The Six Systems of Philosophy), where Vedanta is presented as the crown of Indian philosophical thought.

Reflection: The end of scripture, and the beginning of wisdom. Vedanta does not conclude—it awakens.

Vanaprastha: वानप्रस्थ

Meaning: Stage of gradual withdrawal into contemplation; the third of the four stages of life.

Context: Explored in Chapter 19 (The Journey Home), where Vanaprastha is shown as a transition from worldly engagement to inner reflection.

Reflection: When the forest calls, the Soul listens. Detachment becomes devotion.

Vidya: विद्या

Meaning: True knowledge; spiritual illumination.

Context: Appears in Chapters 8 and 15, where Vidya is contrasted with Avidya and shown as the light that dispels illusion.

Reflection: Light that not only reveals, but liberates. Vidya is not accumulation—it is awakening.

### *Closing Note*

*Beyond definition, each spiritual term holds a depth that unfolds with contemplation. If this glossary helps the reader pause, connect, or gain a clearer understanding of the work's spirit, it has served its purpose.*